HAPPY, JOYOUS & FREE

The Lighter Side of Sobriety

BOOKS PUBLISHED BY AA GRAPEVINE, INC.

The Language of the Heart (& eBook)
The Best of the Grapevine Volume I (eBook)
The Best of Bill (& eBook)
Thank You for Sharing
Spiritual Awakenings (& eBook)
I Am Responsible: The Hand of AA
The Home Group: Heartbeat of AA (& eBook)
Emotional Sobriety — The Next Frontier (& eBook)
Spiritual Awakenings II (& eBook)
In Our Own Words: Stories of Young AAs in Recovery (& eBook)
Beginners' Book (& eBook)
Voices of Long-Term Sobriety (& eBook)
A Rabbit Walks Into A Bar
Step by Step — Real AAs, Real Recovery (& eBook)
Emotional Sobriety II — The Next Frontier (& eBook)
Young & Sober (& eBook)
Into Action (& eBook)
Happy, Joyous & Free (& eBook)
One on One (& eBook)
No Matter What (& eBook)
Grapevine Daily Quote Book (& eBook)
Sober & Out (& eBook)
Forming True Partnerships (& eBook)
Our Twelve Traditions (& eBook)
Making Amends (& eBook)
Voices of Women in AA (& eBook)
AA in the Military (& eBook)

IN SPANISH
El lenguaje del corazón
Lo mejor de Bill (& eBook)
El grupo base: Corazón de AA
Lo mejor de La Viña
Felices, alegres y libres (& eBook)
Un día a la vez (& eBook)
Frente A Frente (& eBook)

IN FRENCH
Le langage du coeur
Les meilleurs articles de Bill
Le Groupe d'attache: Le battement du coeur des AA
En tête à tête (& eBook)
Heureux, joyeux et libres (& eBook)

HAPPY, JOYOUS & FREE

The Lighter Side of Sobriety

AAGRAPEVINE, Inc.

New York, New York

WWW.AAGRAPEVINE.ORG

Third Printing 2018
Printed in Canada

AA PREAMBLE

Alcoholics Anonymous is a fellowship of men and women
who share their experience, strength and hope
with each other that they may solve their common problem
and help others to recover from alcoholism.

The only requirement for membership is a desire to stop drinking.
There are no dues or fees for AA membership;
we are self-supporting through our own contributions.
AA is not allied with any sect, denomination, politics, organization
or institution; does not wish to engage in any controversy,
neither endorses nor opposes any causes.

Our primary purpose is to stay sober
and help other alcoholics to achieve sobriety.

CONTENTS

CHAPTER ONE
LAUGHING AT OURSELVES
Recognizing the power of humor in recovery

CHAPTER TWO
EGO TRIPS
AAs on their favorite subject: themselves

CHAPTER THREE
TWISTED
The lighter side of being new to AA

CHAPTER FOUR

ʿBOOTLEGGERS AND TALKING DOGS
The last days of drinking before finding AA

CHAPTER FIVE

ROUNDING UP THE USUAL SUSPECTS
Twelfth-Step calls that didn't quite go as expected

CHAPTER SIX

LIVE AND LEARN
Stuff my sponsor says, and other lessons from meetings and life

CHAPTER SEVEN
NOT-SO-SILENT NIGHTS
Holiday adventures and disasters before and after getting sober

CHAPTER EIGHT
ONLY IN AA
AA characters, AA stories

WELCOME

In the Big Book, just after relaying the story of the "poor chap" who committed suicide in his house, Bill W. talks about all the fun experiences in AA. "I suppose some would be shocked at our seeming worldliness and levity," he writes in "Bill's Story."

AAs do laugh a lot—at themselves, their drinking histories, and their initial stumbles through the Steps. We may not have felt much like laughing in the beginning. We may have been depressed, or physically sick. We may have caused a lot of damage that we knew would take a while to repair. And we may have felt agonizingly lonely.

But the first time we heard someone get up in front of a meeting and share about some embarrassing drinking event—or some embarrassing *sober* event—we couldn't help but laugh along with them. If someone else did what I did and is joking about it now, we thought, maybe I'm not so bad.

Alcoholics "are possessed of a sense of humor. Even in their cups they have been known to say damnably funny things," writes Fulton Oursler, a friend of AA, in the Chapter One story "Charming Is the Word for Alcoholics." "Often it was being forced to take seriously the little and mean things of life that made them seek escape in a bottle. But when they have found their restoration, their sense of humor finds a blessed freedom and they are able to reach a god-like state where they can laugh at themselves, the very height of self-conquest. Go to the meetings and listen to the laughter. At what are they laughing? At ghoulish memories over which weaker souls would cringe in useless remorse. And that makes them wonderful people to be with by candlelight."

"There is ... a vast amount of fun about it all," Bill W. wrote. "But just underneath there is deadly earnestness."

This collection of stories from AA Grapevine shows how, in recovery, AAs have learned to laugh.

CHAPTER ONE

*"My sponsor told me to learn to laugh at myself,
but I don't see anything funny."*

LAUGHING AT OURSELVES

Recognizing the power of humor in recovery

Sometimes there's nothing to do but laugh. We laugh about what we did while drinking, we laugh about our early mistakes and the pain of getting sober, and we laugh at ourselves even now. When one AA accidentally brings a cake with rum in it to her anniversary meeting ("Cake with Punch"), and another almost sets his car on fire while discussing the Steps with his sponsor ("Steps on Fire"), what else could they do but throw out the cake, put out the fire, laugh and move on?

"I learned to laugh again in AA, and when I'm laughing, the whole world seems to smile at me," writes the author of "If You Feel Good, You're Not Normal." "The laughter in AA attracted me from the very beginning."

Laughter may not be the first key to getting sober, but laughing at our mistakes is just another way we begin to accept ourselves as human.

CHARMING IS THE WORD
FOR ALCOHOLICS
July 1944

D own at the very bottom of the social scale of AA society are the pariahs, the untouchables and the outcasts, all underprivileged and all known by one excoriating epithet—relatives. I am a relative. I know my place. I am not complaining. But I hope no one will mind if I venture the plaintive confession that there are times, oh, many times when I wish I had been an alcoholic. By that I mean that I wish I were an AA. The reason is that I consider the AA people the most charming in the world.

Such is my considered opinion. As a journalist it has been my fortune to meet many of the people who are considered charming. I number among my friends stars and lesser lights of stage and cinema; writers are my daily diet; I know the ladies and gentlemen of both political parties; I have been entertained in the White House; I have broken bread with kings and ministers and ambassadors; and I say, after that catalog, which could be extended, that I would prefer an evening with my AA friends to any person or group of persons I have indicated.

I asked myself why I consider so charming these alcoholic caterpillars who have found their butterfly wings in Alcoholics Anonymous. There are more reasons than one, but I can name a few.

The AA people are what they are, and they were what they were, because they are sensitive, imaginative, possessed of a sense of humor and an awareness of universal truth.

They are sensitive, which means that they are hurt easily, and that helped them become alcoholics. But when they have found their restoration, they are still as sensitive as ever; responsive to beauty and to truth and eager about the intangible glories of this life. That makes them charming companions.

They are imaginative, and that helped to make them alcoholics. Some of them drank to flog their imagination on to greater efforts. Others guzzled only to black out unendurable visions that rose in their imagination. But when they have found their restoration, their imagination is responsive to new incantations, and their talk abounds with color and light and that makes them charming companions, too.

They are possessed of a sense of humor. Even in their cups they have been known to say damnably funny things. Often it was being forced to take seriously the little and mean things of life that made them seek escape in a bottle. But when they have found their restoration, their sense of humor finds a blessed freedom and they are able to reach a god-like state where they can laugh at themselves, the very height of self conquest. Go to the meetings and listen to the laughter. At what are they laughing? At ghoulish memories over which weaker souls would cringe in useless remorse. And that makes them wonderful people to be with by candlelight.

And they are possessed of a sense of universal truth. That is often a new thing in their hearts. The fact that this at-one-ment with God's universe had never been awakened in them is sometimes the reason why they drank. The fact that it was at last awakened is almost always the reason why they were restored to the good and simple ways of life. Stand with them when the meeting is over, and listen as they say the "Our Father"!

They have found a Power greater than themselves which they diligently serve. And that gives a charm that never was elsewhere on land and sea; it makes you know that God Himself is really charming, because the AA people reflect His mercy and His forgiveness.

FULTON OURSLER

MY FATHER'S LEGACY
March 1964

I had a wonderful father. I was his only child. In 1907 my father sent for me and said, "I'm going to die and I've nothing to leave you. You've got to get out into the world and make your own living. How are you going to do it? You're nothing much to look at, never will be. You've no name. You haven't any money. But I am going to leave you a legacy. It's three simple rules. If you follow them, the world will be your oyster.

"First, never be afraid of 'they.' People are more afraid of 'they' than anything else in the world. Strong generals with great armies will face courageously the most outrageous foes yet be terrified of what 'they' might say, 'they' might do, 'they' mightn't like.

"The second rule," he said, "is even more important. Never collect inanimate objects. You can't do it, for they collect you." So, I thought, the more you own the more you are possessed; therefore I own nothing except absolute essentials. I've been as free as air, and it's wonderful.

And the third one, which suited me rather well, was, "Always laugh at yourself first. Everybody has a ridiculous side and the whole world loves to laugh at somebody else. You do the laughing at yourself first and their laughter falls off as harmlessly as if you were in golden armor."

ANONYMOUS

STEPS ON FIRE

August 2007

L ast March, I was driving, smoking a cigarette, and talking to my sponsor on speakerphone. I like to multi-task. We were discussing the fact that I had not yet started working on the Steps. I chucked my cigarette out of the window, closed it, and continued the conversation. Thirty seconds later, I smelled what I thought was a house fire.

Little did I know, but the fire was not outside; it was under my seat. Soon, I saw a slow column of smoke rise from between the two front seats. My sponsor rambled on about the Steps. I interrupted him and said, "I think I'm on fire!"

"Great!" he said. "It's about time you had a fire under your butt."

"No, I really do—my car is on fire!" I said.

"Pull over and put it out," he instructed.

"With what?" My eyes were drawn to the cup of coffee left over from my AA meeting the night before. I grabbed it, poured it on where I thought the fire was, and started to laugh. Fire out, I thought. I began thinking that this was some kind of sign. My sponsor yelled for me to get into the back seat and make sure that the fire was out.

What I found next was chilling. Papers were still burning under my seat. Among them was the pamphlet about the Twelve Steps that my sponsor had given to me a few weeks before. I said, "The Steps are burning!" Squelching the rest of the fire, I rescued that pamphlet; it was a little burnt, but had survived.

"You better believe they're burning," he said. He told me that I had just been abruptly visited by a Higher Power.

"You think?" I asked. It only took me a nanosecond to believe that this was clearly a sign from above. Then I drove home, still shaken by the experience.

My Higher Power happened to come in the form of a cup of AA coffee. If I keep him close, he will be there to put out the fire. For me, there are no coincidences—there is a reason for everything. Since AA is my Higher Power, God as I understand him is always with me in the car. I look at that cup of coffee and smile.

But, to this day, while I usually have a cup of coffee with me in the car, I keep a fire extinguisher in the trunk.

CHRIS M.

CAKE WITH PUNCH *(from Dear Grapevine)*
April 2009

In May, I moved to South Philadelphia. August 22, I was planning to celebrate 28 years of sobriety by telling my story at my meeting. I saw it as an opportunity to get better acquainted. I wanted to make a good impression, so I ordered a big, beautiful cake. Imagine my surprise when, as the cake was being cut, someone said, "I smell rum!" Sure enough, the bottom layer was soaked with rum. The bakery hadn't told me! Of course we were all shocked ... me the most. And then came the laughter. I recognized my HP's humor in this. Once again, he brought my ego down to right size as only he can.

ANNE C.
Philadelphia, Pennsylvania

HEARD AT MEETINGS:
"THERE ARE JUST TWO THINGS AN ALCOHOLIC DOESN'T LIKE—THE WAY THINGS ARE, AND CHANGE."
ANONYMOUS, MARCH 2008

IF YOU FEEL GOOD, YOU'RE NOT NORMAL

April 1976

To my surprise, I have discovered that writing about depression can be quite depressing. But does it need to be? If I give it the light touch and dwell on self-help, rather than on dismal personal experiences, it may not be so depressing.

First, I want to make it clear that I am not an authority on the subject. After extra research, I'm not surprised to learn that some depressions are almost all physical, while many are caused by a combination of factors. Perhaps, like alcoholism, they can be mental, physical, and spiritual. For people suffering some kinds of depression, professional help is absolutely required. For others, I would like to share some of the antidepressants that work for me.

I now realize that my fall from the acute pink-cloud stage after a few months in AA was perfectly natural. Reality is not up in the air someplace. But later I found it hard to understand why the AA program, which had rescued me from the dread and incurable disease of alcoholism, did not relieve my depressions, blues, or blahs. I tried more inventory, attempted more meditation, revisited Step Three, all to no avail. I attended more meetings and found that they helped if they were jolly and full of laughter. Twelfth Step calls helped me to get out of myself only temporarily; sometimes, I couldn't seem to reach people.

The negative feelings were still restless, especially at night. I could not find any reason, except perhaps that my old negative ways of thinking had come home to roost. Or was it too many great expectations, or a sense that time had run out and I was not a success yet? Or was it anger turned in on myself and guilt for all these reasons? I asked for help from my Higher Power, but there seemed to be a block.

One day, I picked up the daily paper and found an article entitled

"If You're Feeling Good Today You're Not a Normal Person." The article
said, "Feel pretty good today? ... If this is true, the Office of Health
Economics wants you to know your condition is 'highly abnormal.'"
Enjoying "complete physical, mental, and social well-being" was said
to be definitely abnormal.

In my own words: If you think you are 100% well, boy, are you sick!
Suddenly, I found myself laughing helplessly. To think that all the
times I felt blue and depressed, I was merely being normal! I began
to wonder whether it had been a mistake to take Step Two. I might be
restored to sanity and become *normal*—and miserable.

Another title caught my eye: "Bruxism." That means grinding your
teeth in your sleep, and the results are a painful mouth and puffy eyes.
(If you are married, I suppose the teeth-gnashing also makes you very
unpopular with your mate.) The causes are depression, strain, and
repressed and controlled anger; overcoming these brings relief. I suffered them all, but I called it alcoholism, not bruxism. However, I did
engage in a lot of figurative teeth-gnashing at the world in general and
people in particular.

Until that time, I had not realized that my sense of humor was at
a low ebb. I was taking myself too seriously. I'd also left a lot of gaps
in my inventory. My vices and virtues were all mixed up. I now realize that I may never know all the reasons for my depressions. But I
can turn them over, whatever they are. Before I go to sleep, I can ask
my Higher Power to help me awake free of them. At first, it seemed a
little strange not to feel depressed or to be thinking negatively. I was
depressed over *that* for a time.

Gloom, depression, and negativism are terribly contagious. In their
grip, I hurt others as well as myself. I made dumb decisions and refused to act when I should, just as I did when drinking. But laughter is
also contagious, and so is good humor. They are part of being restored
to sanity. I can see myself as I really am and become willing to help
myself and to accept help from others. The ability to laugh at myself
restores my capacity to be honest.

Even Thomas Edison had his low moments. It is written that he had a card on his desk reading: "When you are down in the mouth, remember Jonah; he came out all right."

Once more, I have come to believe that the AA program and especially the Twelve Steps can work for my depression as well as my alcoholism. I marvel that, for me, alcoholism and depression have much the same symptoms.

It is no wonder that the laughter in AA attracted me from the very beginning. The restorative power of laughter should never be underrated. I learned to laugh again in AA, and when I'm laughing, the whole world seems to smile at me. I have come to believe that I am being restored to sanity when my sense of humor is restored and I cease to take myself too seriously. I have only to turn my life and my will over to God—and my depression, too. AA is the most effective antidepressant I've found.

Of course, if that article I quoted from is correct, I'm not normal, because I am so happy in AA. Most of my AA friends won't know the difference. Anyway, I've been warned that if I ever do get well, I'll probably lose all my friends.

M. U.
Brighton, Colorado

⌢BUT IS IT FUN͡NY?
November 1953

One thing really distinguishes the alkie ... and that is his sense of humor. It is a particular sense of humor, a nice sense of humor in which he himself is the source, the butt, and the main theme of the fun. He sustains himself—and alkies— with the anecdotes of his alcoholic insanity. He finds no shame in telling of the hidden bottle, and how he ran out of hiding places. Yes, it's true. We all recall the desperate search for a new hideout, how we explored and exhausted the woodshed, the hydrangeas, the old coats at the back of the cupboard, the unsuspected privacy of the water meter, the cistern. We were so brilliant at times we figured we should have taken up chess; we knew so many moves. We'd trick 'em by leaving the bottle in an obvious place this time, behind the settee or the couch, behind the books. Brilliant, until we were confronted with the damn thing.

More desperate, however, was hiding too cleverly; hiding it and forgetting where we put it. It wasn't the kind of thing you could ask the members of the family about. And you couldn't afford to look as if you were looking either. It was really a desperate business. No sport in the world carried so many hazards, anxieties, memory tests, pitfalls, rewards and failures as "Hunting the Bottle." Remember how you'd plant a choice bottle of old low grade tawny in the bush, no cork, you were even afraid of the cork squeaking. Remember going to it like a homing pigeon in the morning and finding it fallen over … drained! Sunday morning it was, too. The outlook was bleak … desperate … the eyes were hot, Mum was cold, your hands were trembling, Mum was solid … you were suicidal. But never forget finding the bottle; never was the reward of inner exultation so great. Remember how we'd grasp the bottle, trembling with cold hands, talk to it, almost sing a paean of praise … mumble … joy … a friend at last … the bottle … the gulp … the splutter … and how lovely when it was inside, giving a momentary glow of comfort—our only friend in the world. All this we can laugh at now, so comical it is … too rich for any stage.

We were the clowns in one of life's greatest tragi-comedies. Together we take these things, of which we were once so ashamed, and we hold them against the shabby tapestry of our alcoholic lives, laughing almost hysterically at our insanity. But the beauty of all this … is that we laugh only at ourselves.

Not anyone else!

JIM
Sydney, Australia

CHAPTER TWO

JANUARY 1969

*"Even if my talk doesn't help anyone, it will
do wonders for my ego."*

EGO TRIPS

AAs on their favorite subject: themselves

I t's not easy to admit it, but ego often rears its ugly head. AAs—
newly sober ones as well as old-timers—like to feel they are
important. In "The Best Little Coffeemaker in AA," a member
brings gourmet cookies to his group to show how well he takes care
of them, and refuses to ask for help (that wouldn't look good). In
"Pancake King," the cook at a weekly AA pancake breakfast gets a
lot of praise for his efforts and later finds it hard to surrender his
spatula; no one else does it quite as well.

It's only later they can look back and smile at these behaviors. As we
learn to love ourselves and focus on helping others, hopefully we don't
need to feel so important. Of course, ego still pops up; as with everything, it's progress, not perfection.

PANCAKE KING
October 2010

About six months after coming into AA, I was feeling great. Then, for some reason, I became restless and discontent, and fell off the early sobriety pink cloud—with a loud thump. We were living in Syracuse, N.Y. at the time, and my sponsor Ed suggested I try a few different meetings, and once again stressed the importance of getting involved with AA service. That's when I stumbled into the pancake breakfast meeting one Saturday morning, and my journey to happy sobriety really started.

"Can you cook? Our regular is a no show," asked a very large man holding an 18-inch spatula near my face. Sensing that "no" was not the correct answer, I chirped "yes" and followed him to the kitchen. "We normally have about 50 for breakfast, but this is chip day, so there may be more," he said, as he pointed to the big box of pancake mix and a huge stack of sausage patties.

Fortunately, I was early and had a few minutes to get the batter going and the stove temperature to the point where my first efforts at least looked edible. Regulars soon started to arrive faster than I could crank out the food. I got some much-needed assistance when a couple of other eager newcomers jumped in to help. We soon had a semi-functioning system up and running and the grumbling for more pancakes slowed down.

After the breakfast hour, there was a great meeting, then a huge surprise. Lee E., the group's chair, made a few announcements and finished with "and I'd like to thank Norm and the kitchen crew for a nice breakfast." There was lively applause, and a few said, "Good job, Norm." I could have won the lottery, and not felt better than at that moment! I was only six months into recovery, and this neat group of people was actually thanking me for doing something that had been fun and rewarding!

After the meeting, during kitchen cleanup (the stove and spatula sparkled as never before), Lee asked if I could help the following Saturday. Wow! I could not wait till next week. I was there at 6:30, a half hour before she arrived to open. That started a commitment of more than a year as cook/coffeemaker, which gave me a firsthand taste of the benefits of service. It was a 10-fold return on any effort expended, just as my sponsor, Ed, had promised.

My second Saturday was even better. I'd done some homework with a few cookbooks, and my pancakes were soon golden brown, uniformly sized, and the sausages "just right" by the time members started arriving. Another thank you from Lee, a couple more "way to go's" at meeting's end—a team of wild horses could not have kept me from that cooking job! Within a month or so I had that kitchen humming by 7:30 A.M. In my mind I had become one of the great pancake makers of the century. I freely shared that information at other meetings all over Syracuse. And then ... black Saturday.

It all started when I took a two-minute break from my post as head cook to refill my coffee. Returning to the kitchen, I was shocked—Dirk had taken over my spot! He was using my spatula to turn pancakes on my stove, and had moved the pancake batter. Silently furious, I deferred to his seniority (he had over a year in AA at the time), and I took the demeaning position of juice pourer, mentally recording every mistake he made. When Lee thanked us that morning, I was very embarrassed, as many of Dirk's pancakes were the wrong size, and several of his sausage patties were burned. I sensed my reputation going up in flames.

An urgent meeting with Ed was called for. I vented my anger over Dirk's pushy ways as Ed looked at me with bemused patience. He told me not to take myself so seriously, let it go, and keep on with my duties at the pancake meeting. It would all work out. He repeated that I always tried to play the big shot, and reminded me that I had a tendency to pole vault over fly droppings. "Your childish ego is getting the best of you—again," were his parting words that morning. Now I had two resentments—Dirk and Ed.

I was able to solve the problem the following Saturday, and thereafter. As soon as I arrived at 6:30 A.M., the spatula never left my hand during the breakfast hour. I also had a new guy I was sponsoring bring my coffee refills to the stove, so no one could intrude on my command post. I don't think I bothered to tell Ed about my creative solution. Ego aside, it was an important time in my recovery. Arriving early, I got to know some of the group members well, and made some friendships that continue to this day. The commitment and responsibility needed to do that job carried over into other parts of my life, and I became a better husband, father and employee. If I could keep the stove and spatula clean, maybe I could help my wife around our kitchen. If I could bite my tongue at Dirk's intrusion, perhaps I could be more patient with my kids. And if I could listen to Ed, maybe I could lighten up on myself and those around me.

After about a year as pancake king, my son started playing in a youth hockey league, and I volunteered to help with team practices. Our ice time at the rink was Saturday from 7 to 8 A.M., so I reluctantly gave up my important position at the meeting. To my surprise, I found myself as responsible around the practice rink as I had become at the pancake meeting. A few of the good habits developed as cook/coffeemaker found their way to my role as a father. A nice surprise.

After the four-month hockey season ended, I returned to the pancake meeting. I was fearful that it may have closed down, since I had not been there to run the place. Surprise ... it was bigger than ever! And during the thank you's at meeting's end, it was never once mentioned that a former celebrity cook was in the room! Hard to believe. But by this time my ego had been downsized just a little, and both Ed and I got a chuckle out of Lee's oversight.

Many other service opportunities have popped up over the years, always a return far in excess of effort expended. A while ago, my wife Lesley and I went to a meeting we hadn't attended in a while. We learned that the coffeemaker had not shown up the preceding week, attendance was dropping, and the meeting was in danger of closing. She volunteered us to take over the coffee duties, and within a short time, the meeting was back on its feet. No applause this time, but it was a great feeling to see energy come back into the room and enthusiasm return. Once again, an outsized reward, which I now believe to be the norm for AA service opportunities.

We moved to North Carolina three years ago, but I often smile when I think of my first service opportunity at the pancake meeting. I have also been fortunate to locate many other chances to help in the program over the years, such as coffeemaker at many different meetings, a couple of group secretary spots, several treasurer posts and GSR; and I have been privileged to sponsor quite a few men. All have been important in my recovery, and rewarding far in excess of any effort on my part.

I was told early on you can't keep it if you don't give it away. For me it's a privilege to be part of this wonderful Fellowship. It has been an even greater privilege to have been involved with any AA service. I was told as a newcomer to not drink, go to meetings, work the Steps, and get involved—wonderful advice that has led to a great life.

NORM H.
Cary, North Carolina

ᐸBRIGHT LIGHᕔS, ᐸBIG EGO
September 2004

M y first attempt at sobriety was back in 1988. I went to meetings every night, I read the Big Book, I prayed. I, I, I ... You see, even though I prayed to God I really felt as though I was conquering all my problems by myself. I lived in a community called Montego Bay. I didn't drive, so friends took me to and from meetings. On one particular night I was very discontented. I didn't care for anything said at the meeting and all the way home I questioned why I was even bothering to stay sober. Then something miraculous happened as we approached the "Montego Bay" sign—the light bulbs started to burn out. The only part of the sign left burning was "ego." No one but me seemed to notice, and I took it as a sign from God. My ego had been edging God out and my pride and self-centeredness were blocking my serenity. My night immediately changed for the better.

CAROL T.
Bishopville, Maryland

ᴛHE UP-AND-ᴅOWN EGO
August 1978

To set the scene properly, I'll have to confess that I am an inmate in a womens' prison. In the dormitory where I lived at first, there was a group of women, early risers, who would meet in the dayroom every morning and have a cup of coffee and a little idle chatter before going to work.

After several months of incarceration, I began noticeably losing the weight I had gained the year I was free on bond, and I was beginning to look much better. Also, I was becoming more adjusted to my surroundings and was less tense. These little coffee gatherings were usually pleasant, and we were usually generous with compliments to each other, if only to bolster morale.

Then, suddenly, I began receiving insults instead of compliments. After I had lost twenty-five pounds, one woman began making little remarks such as "You're not gaining weight, are you?" At first, I let the remarks roll off my back, but then she zeroed in and began criticizing the fact that I put on makeup. Then she would say, "Gee, since you've been in here, you've aged ten years." After a couple of weeks of persistent early-morning insults, I decided to drink my morning coffee in my room. Prison life is discouraging enough.

The insults had taken their toll, though, and I became concerned that perhaps I had, indeed, lost my looks. I watched for new wrinkles in the mirror, and I made a daily figure inventory in the full-length mirror to make sure I wasn't gaining weight. I was still losing—probably from worrying. My ego was in a slow healing process, after being severely devastated, and any kind of slight had an effect way beyond proportion. One snide remark would ruin my whole day. Then, one Sunday, some visitors from the free world—two women and two men—came to visit our AA group. They made a big fuss over me, because they had heard that I had written an article for the Grapevine, and it had been accepted ("My Name Is Helen," July 1977). Before the meeting started, I sat with these visitors and had a delightful conversation. I must admit that being singled out really made me feel pretty good.

When the meeting was called to order, I took a seat in the front row with the other inmates. I was facing the table where the guests were. One of the men—I'll call him Joe—kept smiling and looking at me. The other three visitors spoke, and all the while they spoke, Joe kept smiling and watching me. I began thinking that maybe I didn't look so bad after all, and I would flash him my prettiest smile when our eyes met. I began to feel pretty darn good—made sure my blouse was buttoned, though, and made sure my skirt was properly tucked in. I began to feel color rising in my cheeks as this man continued staring at me.

At last, it was Joe's turn to speak. It was pretty obvious that he picked me out of the crowd to talk to, and he kept his gaze on me, kept smiling. I nodded when he said something heavy. I laughed merrily when he said something funny. All the time, in the back of my mind, I was tickled pink because my tormentor was there, and Joe clearly thought I was attractive, whether she did or not.

Joe began wrapping up his talk, still watching me, still smiling, while I basked in his attention and felt all puffed up. Then he related the incident that had cost him his eyesight some years ago. Joe was totally blind.

It was all I could do to keep from bursting out laughing at myself. That meeting brought things back into perspective for me.

H. P.
Florida

THE BEST LITTLE
COFFEEMAKER IN AA
February 1988

"AA doesn't work for me," he said. "It doesn't work for me, either," I replied. My new friend was not in the best of shape. He was just leaving the hospital. I was helping him fill out some forms, since that's part of my job. There was an element of life that was missing from his eyes. He was thin, as if he had starved for a long time. Whatever they had put him in the hospital for, he looked like a man who was starving to death. Not just from lack of food, but from a spiritual starvation.

Worst of all, he looked like someone who had seen or heard nothing humorous for years.

But he raised his head and stared at me. I could tell he was surprised by my answer. So I grinned, because he was looking directly at me. It was the first time he had done that. Then I told him the story of "When I Was Coffeemaker."

"I was railroaded," I told him. "Forced into it against my will. By the way, how many AA meetings have you been to?"

He shrugged. "I dunno. Maybe a dozen. But it doesn't work for me."

"Me neither," I repeated.

I was coerced forcibly into the job of AA coffeemaker (I explained to him). Now, this was one of your big meetings—usually about eighty people or more. I was nominated and voted into the office by acclamation—no one chose to run against me. A great honor! Well, I decided to show them how tough I can be. I accepted. But I'll tell you, a week later I got even with the guy who nominated me. I talked him into being my sponsor!

Now, you might think it's easy making coffee. It ain't. It's hard. Especially when you're doing it for eighty, ninety, maybe a hundred alcoholics, the same ones every week, and they don't show any appreciation. Let me tell you, it's no picnic.

This meeting started every Friday at 6:30 P.M., which was about two hours after I got off work, on the other side of town. That meant I had to drive all the way over there and do the job without even going home first. Not only that—I had to stop on the way over to buy fresh coffee cake at a bakery. This was not one of your stale cookies meetings—it had class. None of that nondairy creamer, either. I used to buy real cream. And the coffee? Of course it had to be the best in AA. I wanted to show these people I could take anything they could dish out.

I found a produce store that sold gourmet coffee and bought five or six pounds at a time. I tell you, people started begging me for the secret.

Now that wasn't all, my friend. Not only did I have to make two big urns of coffee and hot water for tea, I also had to set up these huge tables for the entire room, line up all the chairs, set out the free literature, and get the stuff ready for the secretary. Not only that, I had to get all this done before anybody else showed up. After all, I didn't want anyone saying I had help, did I? Oh, and then after the meeting I had to put all the tables and chairs back where they came from and wash the coffee urns. It was hard trying to stop people from helping with clean-up, so I finally had to accept that.

Well, to make the story short, I resented this job every week for six solid months. It never occurred to me that there might be something wrong with my thinking. But I was determined to show them. I turned up every week, cold sober. Of course I knew that when the time drew near for my term of office to end, I had them where I wanted them. Because by that time, I had the job down pat, you see. On Valentine's Day I brought heart-shaped cookies. On St. Patrick's Day I got green cookies shaped like shamrocks. I knew where to get the best deal on freshly baked coffee cake, and once a month I brought in a huge birthday cake. I knew exactly how to set up all the chairs and tables in the least possible time to seat the greatest number of people in the smallest possible space. And no one else knew these secrets, because I was doing the whole job alone. In other words, this meeting had become entirely dependent on one person—me, the coffeemaker. Well, I figured I had the perfect revenge. All I had to do was wait until my very last week as coffeemaker. Then I stood up and announced that my job was finished. They hastily elected some poor newcomer to take my place, and I handed over the keys. But I knew I wouldn't be back next week. There wouldn't be anyone to train this poor sucker—he'd just have to figure it out himself. He'd probably quit when he discovered how much work was involved. There was no way they'd ever find a replacement for me. And with no one there to set up the chairs and make coffee, I figured this meeting would last about a month before it went out of business entirely.

However, there was one thing I hadn't quite figured on—that I would actually miss that stupid job. I was true to my resolution and stayed away from that meeting (I kept expecting to hear reports that it had folded for good). But now I suddenly found that I missed having something important to do on Friday evening.

I also realized something I hadn't really thought about: I had somehow stayed sober for the last six months. Maybe this had something to do with the fact that I was forced to think about someone besides myself for a while. Maybe I had approached that coffeemaker job with as warped and twisted a mental outlook as I had ever been able to manage when I was drinking. But I had shown up, and I had done it, and I was getting better. Not only that, I was even beginning to make friends, and people were speaking to me and remembering my name.

HEARD AT MEETINGS:

"I HAVE TO DO THINGS THAT GET MY MIND OFF MYSELF AND OUT OF THE CENTER OF THE UNIVERSE. IT'S TOO CROWDED, ANYWAY."

—JIM F., TASMANIA, SEPTEMBER 2008

Maybe "it" was working in spite of myself.

Well, it wasn't long before I found myself another AA service job, as secretary of a different meeting. Ever since then, I've had at least one job where I have to show up on a regular basis and think about somebody besides myself.

You see, that's why I said that AA doesn't work for me. Because it's the other way around. I *work for AA*. If I don't work, I don't get better. There's no recovery without service.

What's that? You want to know what happened to that meeting after I deserted it? Oh, I went back a few weeks later just to see how far downhill it had gone. Let me tell you, it was awful. This guy who replaced me as coffeemaker didn't have the least idea of the right way to set up the tables and chairs. So they got set up any which way. Needless to say, the quality of the coffee left a lot to be desired. Worst of all, the new coffeemaker was getting there much later than I ever did. Which meant he didn't have a chance to do it all by himself—other people were helping. It was almost like he was cheating. I was scandalized.

But somehow, the meeting managed to continue without me. That was a couple of years ago, and now I'm General Service Rep for that same group. We've gone through several other coffeemakers by now, and I'm damned if every one of them doesn't take that job as seriously as I did. But then, this sobriety stuff is a serious business, isn't it? Say, what are you laughing at, anyhow?

BART B.
San Francisco, California

MY ICED TEA FIT
September 2009

"Lesley, will you get me some iced tea!?" I shouted from my recliner, with my right knee on a pillow following knee surgery. "Sure," came the cheerful voice of the lovely lady who has put up with an oftentimes demanding spouse for all these years. "Here you go. I'm off to a meeting," she said, handing me the bottle of tea and a glass of ice, then walking to the door.

As I was pouring the tea, it hit me. There were only four cubes in the glass. I didn't ask for room temperature tea or lukewarm tea. I asked for iced tea. As any tea drinker knows, it takes at least eight—preferably 12—cubes to make a good iced brew! What was she thinking?

"LESLEY!" I bellowed, and then saw her car backing out of the driveway. Reaching for my cell phone, my first (alcoholic) thought was to engineer it so that she could come back to complete the assignment ... properly. But just as I was about to hit the call button, the face of my old sponsor, Ed L., came to mind. I could see him clear as day looking over his glasses with a half-smile, slowly shaking his head back and forth.

"Norm, you are such an idiot. With your childish ego, you think the whole world revolves around you and can read your mind. We all should bow to your every whim, do everything exactly as you wish. When are you ever going to learn?"—his often repeated theme.

Putting the phone down, I was reminded that I still try to play the big shot. I want what I want, when I want it, completed precisely as I ordered.

I do know better. But still, the old thinking comes back—in a moment—and often with a lot of force.

It's been a while since my iced tea fit. I was, however, thinking about it recently as I picked up my 32-year chip. The same sweet person who only serves four ice cubes at a time presented the medallion to me in front of my home group. She told them that the man who was within inches of being kicked out of the house all those years back had become a good husband, father and, in more recent years, a caring grandfather. From a bumbling, controlling lost soul, to that meeting, where I stood as a very grateful and ever-so-fortunate member of this wonderful Fellowship, what an action-packed journey it has been! It hasn't been a smooth or uneventful ride, but the progress is there.

I'm moving in the right direction, and feel truly blessed. Two steps forward and then one back seems to be my operating method. I'm still quite demanding, and often childish and ego-driven, even after all these years. When I mess up now, however, I know what to do. I talk to my sponsor, dust myself off and get to a meeting. The transgression is resolved ... until the next time. Progress, and not perfection, that's my goal.

But I know that with the Steps as my guideposts, all the tools we have, and an ever-present HP, I'll be just fine. Thirty-two years ago I was told don't drink, go to meetings, and life will get better. Best advice I ever got!

NORM H.
Cary, North Carolina

CHAPTER THREE

*"Okay! I just finished my ninety meetings in ninety days!
When will you people tell me how this thing works?"*

TWISTED

The lighter side of being new to AA

It's hard to remember, after several years in the program, how confusing it all was at first—figuring out how to work the Steps, learning what the Traditions mean, dealing with that first "drinking event" without a drink, and starting to relate to and trust other people. Members write about their surprise when they realize no one notices or cares that they're not drinking, such as in the story, "How to Act at a Party." Others share about finally finding joy in life. "Among the many things I'd lost by the time I got around to AA was my sense of humor. Now—with fourteen months of dryness and maybe a month or so of sobriety under my belt—some of those things are trickling back," writes the author of "Funny Things Happen." The stories in this chapter are about the missteps, discoveries, and lessons learned in the early days.

LEARNING TO FLY

February 1992

My name is Sybil, and I'm an alcoholic. I got to this Fellowship in 1941, and I want to just reminisce with you a little bit about the olden days, what I call the covered wagon days. A couple of weeks ago, my husband asked me if I could recall my last drunk, and I said, "Yes, I can." I was driving along one day, wanting to go home but afraid to because I couldn't face anyone, and I ended up in San Francisco. Now I couldn't go home for sure—it was the next day. What was I going to do? Shaking, sweating, eyes bloodshot, face puffed up, I'd run out of lies, and I thought, If I go home right now it's going to be too late. I can't think of a lie that will wash.

I parked the car and I walked, and I saw this sign, "Sultan Turkish Baths." I decided I could sweat it out there and get myself in shape, but I thought I'd better have something to read. So I stopped at the newsstand and bought a *Saturday Evening Post*—five cents. It was dated March 1, 1941, and on the cover it said, "Alcoholics Anonymous, by Jack Alexander." I was stunned because I had read about AA in 1939, in the *Liberty Magazine*, I believe, one little paragraph about an inch big. Even that impressed me and I intended to cut it out and save it but I hadn't. But here it was. So I took the magazine with me, had the Turkish bath, and even though I was just too sick to think, I knew there was hope.

I somehow got the impression that there was an AA hospital or clinic or something, but at the bottom of the article it said if you need help, write to Box such-and-such in New York. I rang the bell for the bath attendant and asked for pencil, paper, envelope and a stamp, and I think I wrote a rather pitiful letter to New York. I said, I am a desperate alcoholic and I'll take the next plane back there and take your cure.

The answer came a few days later, airmail special delivery, from Ruth

Hock, God bless her. She was Bill W.'s nonalcoholic stenographer and had been for many years when Bill was in Wall Street. And now she was still working for him and she answered all the mail from that *Saturday Evening Post* article. She answered my letter and said, "You needn't come back to New York, there's one group in Los Angeles. That's for all of California. It's very small and it has been a struggle for them. They have met in a couple of hotel lobbies but they are now meeting in the Elks Temple every Friday night at 8:30." And she said, "You'll be very welcome, I'm sure. They have no women alcoholics in California."

I seemed to have unbounded faith that it was going to be okay. I got dressed, but I couldn't comb my hair so I tied a turban thing on my head and I poked my hair all up under it, and down I went. When I got to the Elks Temple they directed me into a small dining room, and seated around the table were ten or twelve men, and a couple of women. I made myself invisible, if that's possible, because they all looked so happy and were laughing and talking. I thought, Well, they're the doctors and the nurses and so forth, and I thought they would be giving me a pill any minute now—the magic pill, the cure-all.

Eventually a man got up and rapped on the table for order. And he said, "This is a regular meeting of Alcoholics Anonymous in California. We are a band of ex-drunks who gather to obtain and maintain our sobriety on an all-time basis with no mental reservations whatsoever." I thought to myself, What an order; I can't go through with it. Well, I didn't have to go through with it that night. I didn't get a chance because he continued with, "But as is our custom before this meeting starts, all you women leave." And these two women that I hadn't even noticed particularly because I was so desperately frightened, they just strolled out into the lobby. I later found out they were the wives—there was no Al-Anon then, and the women were quite used to leaving the meeting and waiting in the lobby; they came back later for coffee and donuts. But I thought this had been cooked up to throw me out. And it worked, because I put my hands over my face and I ran out into the lobby. I lurked around in the ladies' room awhile and then I went into hysterics and I got in my car and I headed for a bar and I got very drunk.

I thought, How exclusive can you get! To kick me out like that. And as I drank and got more livid, I turned to the people beside me at the bar and I said, "I'm a member of Alcoholics Anonymous." And they said, "So what!" Then at 2 p.m., when the bartender was trying to get me out of there, I called Cliff, who's in the book *AA Comes of Age*. Cliff and Dorothy had been taking care of all the Twelfth Step calls for California since the group started in 1939. I was very indignant. I said, "Well, I went down to your group tonight and they threw me out." He said, "Oh no, no, I'm sure they did not do that. Did you tell them you were an alcoholic?" I said, "Of course not. No, they threw me out all right." He said, "Well, we need you, we need you. Please come back. We haven't had a woman alcoholic." When I heard the words "we need you," I thought, Well, I am a good typist and maybe I should volunteer my services. Then I said, "All right, now, I've had about enough of this and I want you to send your AA ambulance." He said, "We don't have any such thing. You go back next Friday night and tell them you're an alcoholic. You'll be as welcome as the flowers in May."

I don't know what I did that week. Probably was drunk and sober and drunk and sober, but I know this: that it was a miracle I ever went back, and thank God I did. But I didn't go back alone. Because during that week my brother Tex came to see me. He came in the house and he picked up the pamphlet Ruth had mailed me from New York, the only one that AA had. It was a thin pamphlet and gave a few basic facts on the Steps, and as he read it he had a pint bottle in his hip pocket, as usual. He was reading and saying, "That's good stuff, Syb. They really know what they're doing there. So you're going Friday, huh?" And I said, "That's right, Tex." So he says, "Well, I'm going with you." He said, "I'll tell you the truth—the reason I want to go there. Those guys that are working for me down on Skid Row. I can't get a regular crew together." He was a vegetable peddler then, with a truck run around four in the morning, and the winos sometimes didn't show up. He said, "If I can sober them up, I'll make a lot of money. So what I'm going to do is take them all down there and get them all fixed."

So it was with fear and trembling that I looked forward to that Friday night, because Tex pulled up in front of my house in his vegetable truck and standing in the back were eleven winos. I crawled up in the cab of the truck with Tex and down we went to the meeting. There were a few more people there that week, but the full impact of the *Saturday Evening Post* hadn't hit. But I got to hear the Twelve Steps read, and also the fifth chapter.

At the conclusion of that meeting, Frank R., God bless him—he was my sponsor and so was Cliff—reached over and got a bushel of mail that had come because of the article. Hundreds of letters from alcoholics. He looked at that skinny little crowd there with Tex, and his winos, and me, and about fifteen others, and he said, "Well now, we got to get all these drunks down here by next Friday night. So we're going to have to cut this crowd up in sections. And if there's anyone here from Riverside County, come down and get these Twelfth Step calls." Tex went down in front and Frank gave him forty or fifty of the letters to read and answer from alcoholics who asked for help. Then he said, "Anyone from the beaches?" This guy raised his hand, Curly from Long Beach, and he went down and got forty or fifty letters. And this went on—Pasadena, Santa Monica, and one guy from Fresno, one from Santa Barbara and so forth, until there was one remaining stack of letters, about a fifth of them.

And he said, "I've been saving this stack up for the last because we now have a woman alcoholic. Her name is Sybil. Come up here, Sybil. I'm putting you in charge of all the women." I had to be honest. I went up there and I said, "Well, I'll probably be drunk next Friday. I always have been." And then I said, "What are you going to do tonight? What are you going to say to me that is going to make it different? So that when I walk out that door tonight during the week that I'm out there by myself I won't get those butterflies and the sweating palms?" I said, "What's going to be different? You got to do something tonight. How can I stay sober for a week? I'd like to be able to go and ring doorbells and bring all those drunks down here. But I haven't read the Big Book." He said, "I know that."

I said, "Truthfully, I haven't read your pamphlet. I haven't felt well enough to read." He said, "I know that. You're not expected to know very much." But he said, "You asked me how you could stay sober until next Friday. Now I'll tell you, it's in that Big Book that you haven't read. Somewhere in that Big Book it says that when all other measures fail, working with another alcoholic will save the day. Now I'm going to tell you what to do quite simply. You take this basket of mail and tomorrow morning you start ringing the doorbells, and when the girl answers the door you say to her, 'Did you write this letter asking for help with a drinking problem?' And when she says, 'Well, yes I did,' say, 'Well, I wrote one like that last week and it was answered. I went down there and I looked them over. I didn't find out how they're doing it but they're doing it, and they look good. So if you want to quit drinking as badly as I want to quit drinking, you come with me and we'll find out together.'"

"Oh," I said, "I think I can do that alright." So I took the mail and I went home with it, and I was getting ready the next morning to get in my car and start ringing doorbells, and my brother Tex came over. He said, "I'm going to ride around with you for laughs." Well, it wasn't for laughs. We made all those calls and out of fifty we may have gotten a dozen or more. Some of the letters were from landladies who wanted the guy upstairs not to make so much noise on a Saturday night, and sometimes it turned out the wife had written in for a husband who was an alcoholic, and Tex came in handy there. And some of them were from women who wanted help.

We did take a number of women down and a few men. The meeting grew—and I mean it mushroomed. But here's what happened. Frank

HEARD AT MEETINGS:
"THE TROUBLE WITH IMMEDIATE GRATIFICATION IS THAT IT ISN'T FAST ENOUGH."
– RICK W., NEW YORK, NEW YORK, JANUARY 2009

had said, "I'm putting you in charge of the women." Well, to me that was like a neon sign that was going on and off, "charge, charge, charge." And I could be real big because Frank and Mort gave me a notebook and they said, "Now you write down all the names of women and then you get them a sponsor. And you have the sponsor report back to you. Then, when you look in your notebook, you will know who you gave the call to. You'll have the report on it. That's a good system." And I took it oh so seriously because I'd go down to the mother group—now we had two, three, four hundred people possibly, microphone and everything—and as the forty or fifty women came in and they were seated, I could think, "There's Eva. She called on Bonnie. Bonnie called on so-and-so, and Fran, and yeah, yeah." And it checked out perfectly, beautiful. Then I would tell Frank and Mort it was working fine. They'd say, "That's nice. You're doing a good job."

But one night I went to the mother group and a gal came down the aisle and she had six strangers with her and they hadn't been cleared through me. And I walked up to her and I said, "Where did you get these women? You know what Frank and Mort are going to say about the system." She said, "To hell with the system! I have friends who have a drinking problem same as I do, and they found out that I was getting sober and staying sober. They asked me how I was doing it. I told them I joined AA. They said, 'Can I go with you?' I said, 'Yes.'" She said, "It's as simple as that and anytime anybody wants to come to an AA meeting with me for a drinking problem that's the way it's going to be, and I'll never report to you again."

Well, when she told me that, tears came to my eyes and I couldn't get out of there fast enough. I wanted to run up to Huntington Park and tell my brother Tex all about it. But he wasn't there, and you want to know why? He had been excommunicated. Because he had started a group. The powers that be, the boys downtown, called Tex on the carpet and said, "Tex, fold the group up. Where's your loyalty to the mother group?" He said, "I'm loyal to the mother group. I'm just sick of picking up guys in Long Beach and driving them thirty-five miles to Los Angeles, so I started a group at the halfway point. Some of my boys are down here tonight. You come out to our group next Friday night and we'll just kind of visit back and forth." And they said, "No, you're excommunicated," and he laughed and laughed and laughed. About a month later they called him down. They had a committee meeting and they asked if he decided to fold up the group and he said, "Nope. Doing fine. Got a lot of the boys down here with me tonight and you're welcome to come to my meeting. It's a participation meeting where alcoholics all talk." Well, at the mother group, we had two speakers, Frank and Mort, for two years. So they said, "We thought you'd say that, so we have incorporated Alcoholics Anonymous in California." And they had. Those that are still around down there will tell you. It took us about a year to laugh that one off, until Tex began to visit the mother group and the mother group members began to visit the Hole in the Ground Group—it was called that because they met in the basement.

Tex advised me to resign my job of being in charge of the women. He said, "Tell them you're too busy helping your brother with his group and suggest that they have a secretary of their very own." I did that, but how it hurt. But it had been good for me at the time, because I had no ego. My ego had been smashed for so many years, and it was good to feel that I was wanted and needed and that I had this little job to do. It was good for me at the time and it was good that I gave it up.

Several years later, they called me up and told me to come down and be the executive secretary for the Central Office of Alcoholics Anonymous in Los Angeles, and I was, for twelve glorious years. So you see in AA you turn a new page and it's all new again. I want to be a newcomer—this seniority bit is a lot of baloney. We're all fledglings, learning to fly.

SYBIL C.
Los Angeles, California

ADVANCED TECHNIQUES FOR SPONSORSHIP AVOIDANCE
March 1998

When I entered the sanctuary of Alcoholics Anonymous I was full of arrogance, rage, and self-pity. And all of these defects were battling for supremacy. No wonder I stayed confused and combative most of the time.

At eight months sober, I was "fired" by my first sponsor because I had a bad case of the "yes buts." She explained to me that I was interfering with her serenity and if I was not going to follow a few suggestions, then she knew other women who needed her help. She told me that she loved me and hoped that I would find someone with whom I could relate. What I heard was "You're not good enough" and "You've failed to meet my expectations." So I made a point to tell everyone at my womens' meeting how wrongly I had been treated.

Why weren't they getting angry with me? Why weren't they agreeing with me? Why were they laughing?

I've always been able to manipulate people to my way of thinking. But they were taking her side. And why were they offering to temporarily sponsor me until I found a new sponsor? Didn't they know that I wanted them to shun this woman, treat her as an outcast, make her pay for my humiliation?

I've had three other sponsors since then and am just now understanding why my first sponsor had to let go of me. Over the course of six years, I've sponsored several women, and I know how frustrating it can be on this side of the "yes buts" and the excuses.

Here is my list of recommended ways to treat your sponsor if you don't want to develop the level of trust necessary for working a thorough and cleansing Fifth Step with her:

1. Call her after all major decisions in your life and tell her how well you've managed by yourself.
2. Avoid calling her when you feel angry because you know she will help you look for your part in it.
3. Tell her only what you think she needs to hear, omitting the details that you consider unimportant and slanting the story in your favor.
4. Avoid attending meetings where she might be, and tell her that you still go to a lot of meetings—they just happen to be on the other side of town.
5. Call her at home in the middle of the day (knowing that she has a daytime job) and leave a message on her answering machine requesting a call back, putting the "ball in her court" and giving yourself some time to "work it out yourself" (along with a ready-made excuse of "well, I called").
6. Give her credit for all of your new decisions and behaviors, telling everyone that "my sponsor recommends," whether she actually did so or not.
7. Screen your phone calls, answering only those that you are in the mood to talk to.
8. If you don't like the suggestions your sponsor makes, keep checking with other AA members until you find one who gives you the answer you want.
9. Remember the character defects that your sponsor has shared over time and throw them up to her when she's helping you discover your own defects.

These are actual behaviors that I've leveraged against my sponsors over the last six years. Today I know that I am responsible—not my sponsor—for my sobriety. So when I play these avoidance games, I'm only hindering my own growth. I must take an active part in my own recovery process.

My new sponsor and I have been together since April of last year, and I've done two Fifth Steps with her. Much of the discussion during these Fifth Steps has been on the level of expectations and acceptance of my own sponsees. If I allow excuses to interfere with my Twelfth Step work then I'm enabling the fantasy that self-will is sufficient for a happy and sober life.

It's hard to ask for help, but even harder to accept that help and do the action recommended. My favorite phrase in the Serenity Prayer is "courage to change the things I can." It takes courage to admit I'm wrong, courage to agree that my way causes me pain and misery, courage to accept help, and courage to change habits that have been forty-one years in the cultivation.

By practicing courage daily, I gain strength. And now I have the second ingredient necessary for relating to another alcoholic. When I share my experience, strength, and hope with other alcoholics, I make sure I tell them about my first sponsor firing me because I was too afraid to make the necessary changes.

Today, I actively seek out my sponsor at the meetings I know she attends regularly. I make sure that I honestly tell her how I am feeling today. I pick up that one-hundred-pound phone and call her when I'm confused and into self-will. And I try to act on her recommendations even if I'm convinced that they won't work. My sponsor isn't a sounding board, just waiting to catch my whining. She's someone whose sobriety I respect and who has spent more years living sober than I have. She is someone who has what I want—courage.

JACQUI H.
Lago Vista, Texas

ᴛWͮ IS TED

April 2010

Twenty-two years ago I attended my first AA meeting at a rehab. I was 15. My first sponsor passed away, and at age 25 or 26 I asked Tom S. to be my second sponsor. He said I wouldn't want him because he didn't love anyone, and that most people were looking to have smoke blown up their butts.

The Big Book talks of a strange, peculiar mental twist. Well, it was upon these grounds that he accepted me as sponsee. I went into the bathroom during a meeting. I had a weird habit of trying to beat the toilet flushing when urinating. After the meeting, I asked Tom if he ever did that, because we had other odd stuff in common. He laughed uncontrollably and said, "Sure, I do!" He said it must be meant to be and agreed to sponsor me.

After I jumped into the Saginaw River in a drunken stupor, he was the only one who would deal with me; not even my own family would.

My sponsor is a very tough and loving man. When Tom came to the hospital to pick me up, the doctor asked him how he dealt with people like me. Tom asked him what kind of doctor he was, and said he must not be a very good one—alcoholics are sick people, he said.

We left the hospital on Tom's motorcycle. He acted as if he didn't notice that I was wearing a hospital nightgown, boxer shorts and foam slippers. We sped off into the night going 100 mph, laughing, and he told me we were going home. He took me into his house.

That was truly the hand of AA, coming through my sponsor. Now I am learning how to live life without alcohol and be reasonably happy.

JACK B.
Saginaw, Michigan

HOW TO ACT AT A PARTY
June 1960

Y ou've had it. Nasty rumors have been circulating to the effect that you have been seen publicly sober on several occasions. You have been conspicuously absent from certain social functions where once you could have been counted on to make ears as well as welkins ring.

Yes, you've taken the dry plunge. You've been off the sauce for days, even weeks. With a great big boost from AA, you're determined to keep it that way.

Then comes what all AA novitiates like to refer to as the First Big Test. You are invited to a cocktail party, an important one, of course (there are no unimportant cocktail parties), and you and your wife agree it's one of those things you'll simply have to attend. After all, joining AA doesn't mean you have severed your relationship with the Family of Man. You are still a paid-up member of society, if not necessarily in very good standing.

Nevertheless, you begin to stew. How are you going to approach this thing, unaccustomed as you are to letting others do all the drinking? What will good old Ray and Bill and George think when you loom before them—upright and coherent? What will your host or hostess say when you refuse a drink? How are you going to break the news?

The time finally arrives—you brace yourself—you face up to the First Big Test. Heart aflutter, you enter the room where the hostilities are to take place. Your genial hostess, exhibiting a smile that was frozen on her kisser two hours before the brannigan is to take place and won't unfreeze until two hours after it's over, greets you by name as you shuffle in.

"So glad you could come," she lies, extending a pinky and one other miscellaneous finger as she cleverly maneuvers you offstage at the same time. "Step over to the bar and tell Herman what you want."

Zero hour! You blurt out, in what in anticipation had seemed a strong, confident voice, but actually emerges as a hoarse croak: "No, thanks. I'm not drinking any more. You see, I have ..."

Your hostess fixes you with that dread smile, a glazed look in her eyes. "Oh, how interesting," she gurgles. "Well, I'm sure you'll find rye, bourbon, Scotch or vodka over there. Or, if you'd prefer, we have a shakerful of martinis freshly mixed."

Now, if you are 100 percent idiot, you grab the hostess by what would be her lapels if she were a man, and insist on explaining that you don't want *anything* to drink. If you're less than 100 percent idiot, you turn your back and forget her as completely as she has turned her back and forgotten you. You march like a little man straight to the bar. You look Herman right in the eye. In a voice that is neither falsely loud nor sneakily subdued, you say: "Straight ginger ale, please."

Right here you receive what is the first in a series of little surprises, mostly pleasant. For Herman doesn't faint, yell for the cops, quit his job in a huff or poke you in the eye. He pours you a shot of ginger ale. As happens in most cases, this is a scene that will be re-enacted many times in the weeks that follow. You will quickly learn that explanations not only aren't expected, but that they won't be listened to. A few good friends, especially if they have a problem themselves, will show interest, but that's all.

But to get back to the party, even though we haven't been missed. ... You proceed to saunter around the joint, appearing as nonchalant as possible under your freshly assumed sobriety, tossing a hello here and a hiya there.

What follows is mostly negative. Not a sipping soul evinces the slightest interest in the contents of your glass—so long as it is more than half full. People at cocktail parties are more concerned with what's in their own glasses.

You may be a trifle chagrined because no old pal rushes up and yells: "Whassamatter, kid, you're way behind schedule. Usually you're ready to get thrown out by this time!" It will probably prove something of a blow to your pride that not one single, solitary guest of either sex will point a bony, accusing finger at you and shriek: "Look! Looka *him. He isn't drinking!*"

You are in for another surprise. This cocktail party is different from any you have ever seen in your adult life. It's a drag. No bright, quick-witted chap—yourself, for instance—is keeping everyone in stitches with his killingly funny remarks. Oh, there's some jerk who's talking a lot, of course, and everyone is laughing like mad at what he says, but it isn't *really* funny, like at the shows where you used to star.

The girls aren't nearly so attractive as they used to be. They may have the gall to treat you with respect, instead of that casual air of camaraderie they formerly exuded—until you knocked the cup of coffee all over their bright new cocktail dresses.

And the men. Not a very interesting type at *this* party. In fact, they're so dull you haven't any desire to waste your time spinning that very funny yarn you used to tell, with such devastating effect, about your experiences with Blodgett, Dodgett and Fidget, the ad agency you once worked for.

After about an hour, you feel you've paid your dues to this particular segment of society and you toddle on. When you hit the fresh air, it comes as a surprise to learn how sweet it smells.

In the weeks that follow, you'll find a strange disinterest in you and your problems if you have the occasion to visit the Old Familiar Places. The people you were called on to "entertain" for business reasons won't object in the least if you sit there and slop up ginger ale while they down booze—so long as you stay around long enough to pick up the tab. The bartenders you used to patronize will treat you with a new-found respect—you can make book on that.

The bane of every AA's existence, of course, is the over-persistent type. Now, thanks to the widespread publicity given to alcoholics and alcoholism, he and she are becoming almost extinct, but occasionally one runs into a host or hostess who does everything but shove a bottle in your mouth and tilt it upwards in a fatuous desire to demonstrate good fellowship.

One chap has developed a special technique to handle females with an over-developed sense of hospitality.

"I've given up liquor," he solemnly announces, "in favor of a new hobby. I'm taking up sex." With that, he makes a lunge for her.

"It works," he reports. "They never force booze on me anymore. But, you'd be surprised ..."

ANONYMOUS

FUNNY THINGS HAPPEN
December 1982

A mong the many things I'd lost by the time I got around to
AA was my sense of humor. Now—with fourteen months of
dryness and maybe a month or so of sobriety under my belt—
some of those things are trickling back.

For example, I'm occasionally caught with a smile on my face. I
find it possible to laugh at myself. And—at the risk of being sacrile-
gious—I've even found grounds for laughing at AA.

Not that I think AA is any laughing matter. Far from it! I take my
AA seriously. But once in a while ...

About a month ago, I was attending a business convention and I
was in a hospitality suite in a swank hotel and the booze was flowing
freely and memories of days gone by were somewhat overwhelming
and an AA meeting sure wouldn't have done any harm.

"A plain ginger ale," I said in a stage whisper to the bartender.

I noticed a guy at the other end of the bar watching. He held his
glass up in a toast toward me and said, "Easy does it."

I tried to focus on his glass, to analyze the color for alcoholic content from afar. It was impossible to tell. "A day at a time," I said as I
returned the sweeping motion of the toast.

He smiled and edged his way toward me. "First things first," he
said.

"But for the grace of God," I replied, and we both started to laugh
as though one of us had just come up with the punch line of the evening.

We studied the name tags on each other's lapels. Naturally, they
spelled out our names and company affiliations in full. Not much
anonymity there.

"I'm Ed F.," I said, playing out the charade to the last.

"Bob M.," he replied.

We shook hands. We took our ginger ales to a quiet corner. And we had ourselves a real fine little AA meeting.

ED F.
Woodcliff Lake, New Jersey

WHAT DO WE DO ABOUT THE WINE?

August 1964

"Listen," my hostess cried as she burst into my room as I was putting up my hair in preparation for the evening's festivities, "did I remember to warn you about toasting the Queen?"

I put the comb down and turned from the mirror. "No," I said coolly, "you didn't."

We were due to dine at Government House in exactly two hours. Cocktails were to be served at eight sharp, dinner at eight-thirty. Protocol, the life blood of a Royal Crown Colony, demanded punctuality. I was to sit on the Governor's left. I was to address him as Sir First Name and his wife as Lady Last Name. (Mine not to reason why—that is what I was supposed to do.) And if by some terrible fluke of my wayward Yankee unconscious I called the Governor Sir Last Name and his wife Lady First Name—well, after all, I am an American. The Governor had no doubt coped with the Angry American and the Ugly American in the course of his duties. Now he was going to be faced with the Absent-Minded American. (The actual miserable fact was that we would both be very lucky if I remembered *either* of his names.) All this I was prepared for. But nothing had been said about toasting the Queen.

"Well," said my hostess plunking herself down on my bed and narrowly missing my best silk dress, thoughtfully laid out for the evening. "You have to. We all toast the Queen. It's protocol."

I picked up my comb again. "Tell me more," I said evenly, turning toward my own startled reflection in the mirror. I had now replied "coolly" and "evenly" which just about exhausted my repertory of casual offhand answers in moments of rising panic. But apparently they served to reassure my hostess, who couldn't see my face, because she expanded on the dilemma in a calmer voice.

"It's like this. There will be a whole row of wine glasses at your place. The last one is for the port. You can refuse everything but the port. It comes at the very end of dinner. When Sir First Name rises and says, 'The Queen,' you must get up and raise the port to your lips."

I gazed intently at myself in the mirror. "Get up," I mumbled, "raise the port to my lips."

"Take a sip. That's all there is to it. You can do that, can't you? Just one sip?"

I turned to smile at her. "No," I said coolly and evenly, "I can't."

There was a sigh like air hissing out of a balloon as she sort of collapsed over onto my dress. "You can't?" she gasped. "What are you going to do?"

I rolled the last of the hair on the top of my head onto a great, fat curler. "My dear," I said crushingly, "I'll think of something. I've been in much tighter corners than this. You're sitting on my dress." That got her out of the room as I had hoped, but she left with the rather despairing expression of the hostess who wishes she had not undertaken to drag a questionable guest into the higher reaches of society. I turned to the mirror again. My reflection stared at me, round-eyed. "What tighter corners have you been in," I said to me, "and where?"

I remembered my first trip out of the country about ten years ago, also to the British West Indies, and how odd I had felt when a tray of free rum punches had been stuck under my nose by the airplane stewardess, as a sort of preview of hospitalities to come. And how I had asked for, and instantly been served with, a plain fruit punch instead. And how I had told myself to remember always to seek a substitute, so as to be part of the occasion, and not to feel separate and alone. That, I discovered, was the great pitfall for the traveling, non-drinking alcoholic—that circumstances could conspire to make one feel cut off even from fellow tourists. This threat to one's identity had sent some of my fellow AAs flying home ahead of schedule from their longed-for trips abroad, and in other cases had provided the psychological springboard for a slip. But it could be circumvented if one prepared oneself for surprise, instead of being alarmed by it. Enjoyment of travel is openness to surprise, but the AA traveler must combine openness with readiness to cope.

I remembered that first evening in Paris when the waiter recommended the *specialité* and then asked if Mademoiselle wished him to recommend her wine as well. Mademoiselle was ready for the question. She wished him to recommend, instead, some substitute common to French people—some nonalcoholic beverage that could be inconspicuously consumed before meals and in cafés, when neither coffee nor Coca Cola were in order. Was there an acceptable French substitute? *Mais oui.* A natural effervescent mineral water called Perrier is by way of being a digestant and is as common as wine itself in every restaurant and café in France.

I remembered the first evening in Rome finding out that the naturally effervescent mineral water was now to be called Pellegrino. That it was just as common as Perrier in Paris, just as acceptable. I remembered during my most recent trip learning the Greek word for a carbonated cider (better than any soda pop I have ever had in the States and just as common) so that I could go along on even such cruise festivities as the wine festival in Rhodes knowing that I had the name of a substitute ready. I remembered on a pub crawl in London being introduced to a then new beverage which has since become my all-time favorite soft drink—Bitter Lemon. (This is a plug, but I can't help it.)

I could hear myself at AA meetings on my return from these jaunts saying the same two things over and over. "Nobody cares if you don't drink," and "there is always a local substitute." Well, now I had come bang up against a situation in which 1) someone *did* care if I did not drink and 2) there was no substitute. You could not toast the Queen in Bitter Lemon. That was becoming obvious. "I will raise the port to my lips and *not* take a sip," I told my bug-eyed reflection in the mirror. But that stare remained. "You'll be sitting on the Governor's left; he'll notice.

They'll all notice. They'll think you're a Communist, or rude, or something terrible." I looked at myself sternly, "I am not any of those things," I answered, "I'm The Alcoholic American"—there was a new one for the Governor, or maybe not so new. I wondered fleetingly if there was a branch of AA in this particular West Indian island. If only I had bothered to check GSO before I set off in my larky way for my two week vacation. If there were just one other non-drinking alcoholic I could now ask about that moment when the Governor stood up and said, "The Queen." If, if, if. "Just don't tell me you've been in tighter corners than this!" my reflection said by way of a parting shot as I left the mirror.

And then I remembered that hot summer day in the railroad station in Rome. I had been misinformed as to the departure hour of my train for Spoleto and had arrived at the track just in time to see it pull out. I had found that the only other train would necessitate my changing late at night at the Italian version of the Jamaica change-over on the Long Island Railroad. I then lost my temper, burst into tears, and tried to repair to the ladies' room—only to discover that I had to queue up in one line for a towel, another for soap, and a third to gain entrance to facilities that included a wash basin. Since I do not speak Italian, all these discoveries were made through trial and error. But ultimately I wound up facing the old reflection again, tear-stained and rebellious this time. "You need an AA meeting," I told myself on that occasion. And I knew it was true because I wanted a drink.

So I stopped crying and put a new face on and went up to the telephone center to try to put a call through to Spoleto without losing my temper. There, leaning against the wall was an American waiting for his call. He looked familiar. I knew I knew him, but I couldn't think how. Then suddenly I remembered. Before I thought further I said, "Hello." His look was not very encouraging. "I know you from somewhere," I went on lamely.

"Really?" he said in the voice of a man who had been picked up before by lonely American girls and was in no mood for another one. "How do you know me?"

I glanced over my shoulder nervously. How could I tell him? Supposing I was wrong? Supposing we were overheard? He might be embarrassed, furious …Then I thought of a perfect code. "Does the name Lenox Hill mean anything to you?" I asked, using the group label of a large metropolitan meeting.

He burst out laughing. "Oh, I know you," he said, all reserve gone, "You're so and so." There was my AA meeting. We spent the next hour together. He helped me get my money changed, bought me a sandwich, and put me on the train with a few well-chosen words in Italian to my compartment mates to make sure I made my connection. I hadn't felt so looked-after and cared-for since my mother used to give me to the Pullman porter when I took the train back to school.

I could hear myself telling about that strange, blessed coincidence when I got back to AA in New York. Providence, I had called it. One of those AA miracles. Well, I reflected, here and now in February of 1964, in the British West Indies I could use another miracle. Like maybe if the Governor would just forget to toast the Queen …

I had no sooner reached my place at the Governor's left when I perceived that something was terribly wrong. There was no row of wine glasses. There was only one glass. Now what did I do? I looked wildly across the table for my hostess, but a foot-high floral decoration almost totally obscured her. All I could see were her eyes. They told me nothing.

The first course was fish. Wine was poured. I let my glass be filled. Maybe they were going to use this for the toast instead of port tonight. After all, it was a small dinner party. Meat was served. Then more of the same wine. The butler hovered over my full glass. I gave him a frozen smile. He came back in a little while and took my untouched wine away. Well, there went the ball game, toast and all.

Then I noticed that everybody's glasses had been taken away. Dessert came. Then cigarettes were passed. "You can't smoke," my hostess had said, "until they pass cigarettes." Well, she'd been right about that, anyway. Coffee was next, just a demitasse, not enough to do any real good, but better than nothing. "Now," I thought, "the port …" The Governor touched my arm and gestured toward the butler who was standing to my right with an entire trolley full of liqueurs.

It'd been a long time since I took a really good look at a collection of after-dinner drinks, but in one glance I could see there was no port. Perhaps, I surmised, we were to toast the Queen in liqueurs. The Governor, who was served first as the representative of the Royal Family, had taken brandy. I smiled frozenly at the butler again. He smiled back. I pointed to the green mint. He poured me one of those little thimbles full, put it at my place, and moved on. I glanced toward my hostess. Obviously I had made the wrong move. Her eyes blinked disbelievingly across the hedge of flowers at me. This time I could read her look. It was quite clear that she thought I had cracked under the strain and taken to the bottle. I tried to wink reassuringly. She shut her eyes in pain. The Governor drank his brandy. Everybody else drank his. Only my little green glass remained untouched. The Governor looked at it and then at me. My frozen smile had now become permanent. If they were waiting for me to finish my liqueur before they passed the port we would sit there until doomsday. I considered dumping it in the flowers, the fingerbowl, over my left shoulder. If only the butler would take it away. ... The Governor seemed unable to look at anything else. I thought that in one more minute I would lean toward him and say, "Sir What's Your Name, Governor dear, I regret exceedingly that I find myself quite unable to drink this spiked green mouthwash. But I have never liked it, and if I ever have to go, I will not go on *crème de menthe*. Protocol or no protocol, Queen or no Queen."

But suddenly the Governor and his lady, as if at some secret signal, rose simultaneously from the table. The Governor's wife started to lead the ladies out of the dining room. I was the first to follow, dazed, unable to believe my reprieve. As she took my arm, I blurted out the question that was uppermost in my mind. "What about the toast?" I asked.

"What toast?" she smiled sweetly.

"Well you know," I fumbled, "The Queen."

The Governor's wife laughed. "Oh, we don't bother with that when we're informal ... and when there are mostly Americans." She peered at me kindly and added, "I hope you weren't disappointed."

I tried to suppress a sudden, hysterical fit of giggles. "No!" I said, "just surprised—surprised is all."

Which brings me back to my starting point—the one fixed element of travel is surprise. The next morning when, as usual, I was awakened by the glare of the sun on the Caribbean, I remembered a promise I had made to the editors of the Grapevine to write a travel piece for other wanderers in our Fellowship. What a perfect day to begin it! I opened my typewriter, put in the paper, and without thinking banged out the title we had agreed upon: "What Do We Do About the Wine?" I stared at it. And then I burst out laughing. I thought of all my pet theories and pat sayings, and the brand names of the better, substitute soft drinks. But my experience of the night before had given me a new insight. When the chips are down, abroad as well as at home, there is only one answer to that old question: "What do we do about the wine?" It can be said in three words. Don't drink it. Pour it in the flowers, in the fingerbowl, over your left shoulder. *But don't, repeat, do not drink it.* One lovely day at a time.

So have a beautiful trip if you're going away this summer. Let no unnecessary worries come between you and your wonderful adventures. Welcome those surprises. *Bon Voyage! Arrividerci!* And, oh yes … "The Queen!"

E. M. V.

CHAPTER FOUR

DECEMBER 1992

BOOTLEGGERS AND TALKING DOGS

The last days of drinking before finding AA

One of the things we laugh about the most in AA is a good drinking story—and everyone's got one, like the story of a visit to a bootlegger described in "The Saddest Story Ever Told," or the tale about a pooch who lectures a drunk about his behavior in "Talking Dog Story." When we tell our stories, the humiliation of remembering things we once did while imbibing is lessened by the spark of recognition in other members' eyes. Here are a few amusing tales of the alcoholic behavior that eventually drove these members into AA.

THE SADDEST STORY EVER TOLD

September 1959

One of the greatest mistakes that can be made by us members of AA is to develop the reputation of being "funny." From the day this idea is conceived you might as well hand in your chips and go home. From that day on everybody expects you to be hilarious, even when you have the most casual announcement to make. To be funny by compulsion is darn near impossible. I know—I made that mistake.

Some many months ago Helen W. of the Grapevine Staff asked me to write an "amusing" article for the Grapevine. I did not know that from that moment on I would be typed as a funny guy. Anything I contribute of a serious nature is met with disbelief and disappointment—and is immediately relegated to the scrap basket. If I want to break into print in the Grapevine (and no one else will have me) I have to be funny or else.

Recently at the North Carolina Convention I saw Helen and again she asked me to "whip up something on the amusing side to add more variety to our usual articles." Being the remnants of a man, I still am unable to say no to a beautiful gal so I agreed even though I doubted my ability to be funny on command.

When I returned home I tried every known means to become funny except resorting to my old formula of what we Virginians call "Giggling Water." Nothing worked. I made faces at myself in the mirror, I repeated some of my funniest jokes and got nary a laugh, I played back some of my talks on my tape recorder and only succeeded in putting myself to sleep. I just couldn't get funny. But I had promised Helen I would send in an article and I cannot get out of it: after all, I'm a Virginian and a gentleman (probably the funniest statement to emerge from this effort) so I will do something funny—I will cross them up and tell them the saddest tale of my sad but eventful life.

This sad story starts during Prohibition Days, and nothing could be more hilariously sad than Prohibition Days. The principal character was I, although I was a character without principle. At that time I was a traveling salesman which reminds me of a funny story that would fulfill the requirements of this assignment but ... no, I must stick to the script and be funny on my own without outside help. I must be amusingly sad.

One of my very best customers was a man who ordered very infrequently and seldom paid for what he did buy except under threat of a lawsuit instituted by our credit department. He was my pet account. He always had an ample supply of apple brandy. The company intimated that I devoted a disproportionate amount of my time soliciting his business.

One morning I called on him and after passing the time of day and ascertaining that he did not want to buy anything and could not pay for what he had bought five months previously, I awaited the customary breaking out of the jug. None came. No good salesman ever allows a call to be entirely unproductive so I bluntly asked Jake about the brandy. He informed me that his car had a broken axle and he had not been able to get up into the mountains to get any.

I assured him that this presented no serious problem, that I had a car with two axles—and we struck off to the source of supply. For about six miles we were on a hard surface road and then we turned off into the mountains. Every road that was uphill and worse than the road we were on was our route. When we neared the top of the mountain the heavens opened and the roads became running streams.

Finally we arrived and the good moon-shiner's wife advised us that her husband was down at the still. We were drenched to the skin by the time we had gone twenty yards down the path where our progress was suddenly interrupted by the twin barrels of a shotgun projecting uncomfortably into my midsection. Jake identified me in time and we completed our negotiations.

I let Jake out at his yard with his two half-gallons and I proceeded on my way with two halves for myself. Immediately out of town I heard the chug-chug of a motorcycle behind me. Yes, it was a state highway patrolman and he followed me all the way to Luray, a distance of at least twenty miles.

My car was covered with mud, a sure indication that I had been up in the mountains. I was driving a coupe and there was no place to hide the jars without stopping the car, which I was afraid to do.

Proceeding down a hill in Luray a car ahead of me was involved in a wreck with a car coming out of a side street. I had to stop. The town cop joined the trooper at the wreck. I did not know whether to stand my ground or attempt to drive around the entangled cars. I had just decided on the latter course of action when the state trooper asked me where I was going. I told him home but he suggested that I might be needed as a witness in the accident. I assured him I had not seen it. He said he had and he was behind me. I told him I had sneezed at the moment of impact and therefore my eyes were closed. My two jars were on the seat in plain view and to my amazement he told me to drive on. Needless to say I did so.

A hundred or more miles and as I approached Fairfax court house a siren blew me down. It was a Fairfax County cop. He asked me why I had passed a car on a hill. As there was only one car in sight and he was going in the opposite direction, I told him I had to pass it or hit it. All the while he was giving my car the once over because of the tell-tale mud. I told him that if he wanted to search my car to take me to the court house where he could search it under the direction of Sheriff Blank or Captain Blankety-blank of the motor patrol. He asked me if I knew these estimable gentlemen and when I assured him they were closer to me than my undershirt, he examined my driver's permit and allowed me to proceed again.

Only sixteen miles now and I would be safely home with my price-less possession. I drove with utmost care and finally pulled into my garage.

Climbing gratefully from the car I removed my suitcase, my briefcase, my portable typewriter and my two wonderful jars. But I am a lazy alcoholic and I did not contemplate making two trips into the house so I gathered them all in my two hands and ... yes, you guessed it. The two jars crashed on the concrete.

Now you have your story—laugh, damn you, laugh.

T. W. R.
Alexandria, Virginia

LEARNING TO WALK *(from Dear Grapevine)*
May 2007

I came to in my walk-in, closet-sized, garage apartment. I blinked and stared at a fifteen-foot aluminum extension ladder wedged diagonally into my tiny room.

Huh? I thought, Jeez, this is getting pretty bad.

When drinking, I developed into a thief. Since I drank every night (and day, if I could), I accumulated a lot of stuff. Whatever I couldn't sell, I kept. It got crowded in my one-room garage apartment. I had bicycles, womens' clothes, barbecue grills, and several tires.

When I dragged myself back to the clubhouse where I occasionally attended meetings, a guy said, "I knew you were drinking again."

"How so?" I asked.

"I was sitting at a red light on Northwest Boulevard about two o'clock in the morning, and you walked by, carrying a big extension ladder," he said. "I didn't think you were working."

The first page of Chapter Three, "More About Alcoholism," includes a line that has always stayed with me: "We are like men who have lost their legs, we never grow new ones." I was still trying to grow new ones. I had been trying for years.

Now that I'm sober a few years, I'm reasonably responsible. I haven't awakened to an aluminum extension ladder, lately.

BILL A.
Iowa City, Iowa

NOBODY'S FAULT (BUT MINE)
November 2003

Forty-five, fifty miles per hour. Three police cars in tow. Lights flashing. Sirens blaring. This old truck I bought for work is perfect—for work. As a getaway car, it leaves much to be desired. I think I'm going to jail. Yet my foggy logic tells me that if I just keep on truckin' like nothing's wrong, those police officers may just give up and let me go on my merry way. (Fat chance!) At any rate, as long as I'm moving, they can't get me.

The police seem to sense that this is my intention. Soon my old truck is surrounded by screaming, blinking police cars. Together, we bump and grind and screech to a halt. I am about to discover just how angry I have made them. Two of the six officers give me a real good, up-close look at their revolvers and "strongly suggest" I exit my vehicle. I answer them with the old "Who, me?" look. They don't ask twice. One of them grabs hold of my hair and drags it out the passenger-side door. Being the obliging fellow I am, I follow my hair. Now blades of grass are poking into my eyes and a long forgotten taste from my childhood returns—the taste of dirt. I have a vague sense that the hand pressing my face to the ground is my own. From this position and in my drunken state, it is impossible to put up any sort of resistance. Nevertheless, to put it mildly, they subdue me for good measure. Cold steel is clamped on my wrists and I'm back up on my feet. Silly me, I forget to duck as I am helped into the back of a cruiser. A bolt of pain shoots through my temple and I collapse on the seat. The door slams shut behind me. Yep, I'm definitely going to jail.

I don't know it yet, but I am the fortunate one. Within the next two years, under similar circumstances, two drunks will be shot to death by police on this same stretch of highway. With those deaths in mind, I am able to look back on my own experience with a little levity and a lot of gratitude. My last drunk, the best day of my life. People raise their eyebrows when I say that, but had it not been for that horrible incident, I may never have found contented sobriety in the Fellowship of Alcoholics Anonymous. It takes what it takes, I'm told. Jail was where I needed to be at that point in my life. To the best of my knowledge, there is no good way to get there.

Those first few days in the police cells were no indication of what was about to happen to me. Miserable, yes, but oddly comforting. At least I was free to wallow in the puddle of bitterness and self-pity I had made for myself, convinced that my life was now officially worthless, equally convinced that the big, bad world was to blame for all of it.

Lucky for me, I had several weeks' convalescence before I had to face the judge. Bail was out of the question, so I was remanded to a correctional facility. That gave me much-needed time to come up with a plan—a plan to get my sorry butt out of jail in the shortest possible time, with the least possible effort. I had bounced around the courthouses enough to know that the judge would not be sympathetic when I informed him that my predicament was all someone else's fault. Surely he would want to see some attempt, on my part, at rehabilitation. I would have to fake it. That meant doing the one thing I swore I'd never do again—attend AA.

I had been sentenced to AA some twelve years earlier after one of my many brushes with the law. I found those AAs to be the most sickeningly happy people I had ever met. I wanted no part of it. After all, every real drinker knows that real AA meetings are nothing more than a bunch of long-faced, ex-drunks who sit around and whine about how they can't drink any longer. They just pretend to be happy to sucker guys like me into enlisting. I attended two whole meetings and left, vowing never to return. Yet there I was, twelve years later, those two capital As my only ticket out of jail. What else could I do? I went to AA.

I had many desires when I walked into that meeting, but not drinking was not one of them. I had no honorable intentions whatever. A pleasant-looking man in street clothes introduced himself to me as Murray and asked me to take a seat. The circle of twenty or so chairs were gradually occupied by inmates who looked about as miserable as I felt. I recall thinking to myself, Now this is AA. Murray opened the meeting and identified himself as an alcoholic. He didn't look to me like the kind of guy who'd ever taken a drink in his life, but who would lie about such a shameful thing?

I heard some sad stories in that room that evening—"My girlfriend ratted me out ..."; "My wife put me in jail, boo hoo hoo ..."—and not a single storyteller accepted responsibility for his own fate. Worst of all, I began to understand that if I were to speak my mind, it wouldn't sound a whole lot different. Suddenly, I didn't want to whine. Then came Joe's turn to share. As Joe looked up from his lap, I saw that besides Murray, he was the only nonmiserable-looking person in the room. In fact, he smiled. Maybe it was just a trick of the light, but he looked—dare I say it?—radiant. When he spoke, he spoke of himself, the wrongs he had committed, his own failings, but all with the unmistakable air of hope. Hope? In this place? I hardly believed my eyes or my ears, yet there it was, of all things—hope. I began to think, I'm in a room full of strangers. What could it hurt to say just a few words? Then, when Murray asked, "Greg, would you like to share?" I ratted myself out. "My name is Greg and I'm an alcoholic." They were the first honest words to leave my lips in quite some time. Next came, "I don't get this God thing."

As AAs are wont to do, Murray gave me the Big Book definition of God, which I still remembered but didn't accept, from those two meetings years earlier. Malarkey, I thought to myself. However, after the meeting, I walked back to my dormitory feeling no ill effects. Considering I'd just sold myself out in more ways than one, I felt better

HEARD AT MEETINGS:
"MY FAVORITE OXYMORON: FUNCTIONING ALCOHOLIC"
– CAROL K., SARASOTA, FLORIDA, OCTOBER 2010

than I'd expected to feel.

Then one evening, a few days before the next meeting, I was sitting on my bunk doing what I did best—pouting, stewing, blaming. Just as those self-defeating thoughts consumed my mind, another inmate tuned his radio to the local FM station. He hung the headphones on his bedpost and sat down to a game of cards. Faint and tinny, the strains of a good, old, heavy metal song wafted across the dorm and penetrated my thick skull. I began to sing along in a whisper: "Nobody's fault but mine/Nobody's fault but—" Kapow! It hit me like a ton of irony. Nobody's fault but mine.

Have you ever been in a room full of criminals, when you're the only one who gets the joke? I burst out laughing and rolled back on my bed. Nobody's fault but mine! I thought it was hilarious, but when I finally came up for air, there were twenty-one pairs of eyes looking at me like maybe I was in the wrong kind of institution. The first sane notion I'd had in years was being mistaken for insanity. I knew instantly that any explanation would be futile. Better to have them think I was crazy than to open my mouth and remove all doubt. I left them all wondering.

I wondered, too, though. It was too real to be crazy. So personal. So profound. What was it? A quirk? Happenstance? Coincidence? None of the words I knew adequately described that eureka moment. It wasn't until much later that I learned that AA's good friend Carl Jung had studied this particular kind of spiritual experience and had given it a name—synchronicity. In short, there are no coincidences. Recognizing the difference, however, requires a measure of open-mindedness. Therefore, I am convinced that, had I not wondered aloud about "the God thing," I would not have been receptive to the response. The Higher Power of my understanding was given meaning that night. In my case, the god of mischief met me exactly where I was at, in a manner that I was willing and able to grasp.

As strange as it felt, things got better from that day on. Among other things, my desire to drink became a desire not to. And for some reason I couldn't begin to explain, I became unafraid to face up to the numerous charges against me. When my court date finally arrived, I stood before the judge and pleaded guilty to every single charge. I told the judge, in all sincerity, that I wanted to change the course of my life. He agreed that that was a good idea and generously sentenced me to four more months in jail, which was a far cry from the two years my lawyer had prepared me for.

That sentence gave me much-needed time to come up with a plan. Not the ulterior sort of plan I'd concocted to get out of jail, rather a plan to stay out. At the top of the list: Alcoholics Anonymous. I went back to the same meeting room I'd shunned twelve years earlier and, boy oh boy, had they changed! No longer were they the sickeningly happy bunch I remembered. Nor were they long-faced whiners. Just a good bunch of people, happy to be free and alive. I am now pleased as nonalcoholic punch to call them my home group. They have given me their wisdom. They have given me their trust. It feels good to be trusted. I try to carry the message as it was carried to me by corresponding with an inmate and whenever possible, by attending meetings at a nearby penitentiary.

As this is a living program, I have also become active in serving my community. After so many years of being a hazard, a public nuisance at best, I feel obliged to do something positive. While I expect there will always be skeptics, I'll continue to strive for respectability in my town. Miracles, it would seem, are not reserved for saints. Thanks to all you anonymous alcoholics, I'm sober and free.

GREG N.
Nipawin, Saskatchewan

HIGHER POWERS AND SLIMMER FIGURES

August 1964

I most certainly believed in a higher power from the beginning. My higher power was called willpower. I figured willpower could get me everything, and I wore it like a yellow ribbon, proudly. I carefully nourished my stubborn willpower in every trifling situation. For example, as a child I suffered from chronic sore throat, but I steadfastly refused to open my mouth so the doctor could swab it. Later in life I reversed this "closed-mouth" policy, and refused to shut my mouth. As a result I found both of my feet in my mouth most of the time. With one foot in your mouth you still have some dignity or at least a leg to stand on. With both feet in your mouth you fall flat on your error. As my mouth always opened automatically when a bottle was passed before it, when my feet weren't in my mouth the bottle was and vice versa.

As time and many, many bottles passed, I not only became drunk but fat! I was in the battle of the booze and battle of the bulge, and I was losing both.

Now, I knew I could stick to a get-thin diet if I called on my old standby, my willpower. I had been on liquid diets before, but I chose the liquids! What a letdown to learn that alcohol contained calories! That my higher power, alcohol, was making me fat! I remembered the time I decided to quit eating altogether and just drink for energy. I asked the doctor why I didn't lose any weight as I was eating absolutely nothing. He explained I had to get the water out of my system first. (What water?)

So I began my diet. Diet foods and no alcohol. These were grim months. Six of them in a row. Willpower prevailed. Truly, I became sylphlike (a worm or grub or an imaginary spirit living in (on) the air,

Webster). I became curvaceous, nasty and very, very thirsty. I also wore a snug-fitting size thirteen and an ugly expression.

When people said, "I believe you are better company a bit plump," I figured it was just envy. When they suggested I was too gaunt and tired-looking I made nasty remarks. I also began reading up on, and expounding on, the Evils of Drink. I became an authority on wet brains, health foods, vitamins and exercise. I managed to let them (my drinking friends) catch me eyeing them oddly as they sipped a cocktail. I never failed to mention their weird behavior at the last party. I became a real Cheerful Charlene at hang-over wakes. I never failed to act cheerful and gay around the hung-over. My favorite expression was, "Sure glad I don't drink." My presence at a party became about as welcome as a scorpion in the baby's crib. I kept careful tabs on the amounts drunk by each one. I not only dampened spirits, I flooded the market. I managed to spoil as many happy drinkers as AA spoils alcoholics. Needless to say, I did not win any peace prizes or the Pulitzer prize for bettering public relations or humanity, that year.

Then one day the power failed. Willpower suddenly took leave-of-absence, and self-pity, resentment, imagination and a doozy of a thirst came to baby-sit with me. Surely I deserved a little social drink now and then. My willpower was functioning perfectly, I'd proven that. Being all dried out so long, I probably wouldn't need much to drink. Besides, I needed to make a lot of amends and get my friends back, didn't I?

Alas, all my thirsty little pink taste buds sprang to life with the first drink. Not only was I thirstier than before, but what an appetite! Even food I had detested tasted like a Parisian chef's delight. White bread was like angel food cake. The more I drank the more I ate. In no time I became my old fat, gay, drunken self. I started bursting out laughing again at everything and anything, and bursting out of my new size thirteen at the same time.

Oh where, oh where was my old dependable willpower? Finally, I called AA. Now I have a more reliable power—God Power. My old higher power which was alcohol has been replaced with God as I understand him. This was a good deal.

P.S. I wear a size sixteen again, but sobriety fits all kinds and sizes, wears well and is most becoming to "lady" alcoholics. Shop around at AA meetings and you'll find just what you're looking for in the line of sobriety.

M. U.
Boulder, Colorado

SELF-DIAGNOSIS: DRUNK
October 2007

So I was an alcoholic! Who would have guessed? Apparently, I was the only one who didn't. Yet, despite my lone surprise, I embraced my newfound discovery with gusto.

I threw myself into the program and did everything that the AAs suggested over the next 89 days. They said, "Go to meetings the way you drank." So I did—in the evenings, right around happy hour. It had been my time to let down my hair at some unsuspecting bar. Instead, I went to a meeting. Weekends were troubling for me, too, so I turned to round-the-clock meetings on those days. They also told me, "Read the Big Book," so I diligently scoured the pages, highlighter in hand.

However, something I'd come across at the bottom of page 31 gave me pause. The last paragraph on that page clearly outlines a simple plan for self-diagnosis, encouraging one who may have doubts to step over to the nearest barroom and try some controlled drinking. Of course, I thought, What if I truly wasn't an alcoholic?

Controlled drinking? Could there really be such a thing as that? I didn't think so.

Well, at least not in my experience. I drank with deliberation—I set out to get as absolutely smashed as possible. However, in my defense, and in my seventeen years of drinking, fighting, and wrecking bars, cars, and homes, it had never crossed my mind to attempt to exhibit some semblance of restraint.

Consequently, it seemed I had found a loophole in the permanence of labeling myself a drunk. Armed with a glimmer of hope ripped straight from the pages of the Big Book, I decided that I would take my drinking where no drunk had ever (successfully) gone before: I'd trudge with it down the road of moderation.

I had a plan, which, to me, was a good sign, for no true alkie I'd ever known had a plan. My strategy was this: I'd go to a bar, wait and socialize for fifteen minutes, and then order a beer. I'd sip that beer over the next fifteen minutes, then wait fifteen minutes more before ordering another. This would only go on for a total of three beers. Then, I was to socialize—free of drink—for an entire hour before retiring for my evening drive home—sober.

Soon, the perfect occasion presented itself for implementing my new method of restrained drinking. It arrived on a Friday night in Detroit, where I was moonlighting as a left-winger on a recreational womens' ice-hockey team. The gals always looked forward to the early weekend night games because that left time for after-play socializing.

Since I was in my first ninety days of sobriety and had never played with this particular team before, all were unfamiliar with my former style of drinking. In other words, they were unaware of my dozen-plus years of vomiting, passing out, blacking out, and missing a lot of work days—really not that stylized at all, come to think of it.

But, my past antics notwithstanding, their ignorance of such go-ings-on would be the cement in the foundation of my new design. It meant that whether I succeeded in my quest for lucid interaction, or failed and got miserably drunk—none would be the wiser.

So I set out and immediately hit a snag. I was shocked to find that the waiting between beers ticked by interminably. There were even a couple of times where I stared unblinkingly at the clock, suspicious that its hands were not moving.

And the socializing? What was that all about? Who has conversations just for the sake of talking while in a bar? I simply rolled my eyes and snorted to myself. Clearly, they were missing the entire point of the venue.

But there my teammates sat, laughing and chatting with little heed to their rapidly warming drinks. I was so disgusted that I could barely focus on what was being said. Still, my first beer disappeared much faster than the fifteen minutes I'd allotted myself to linger over it. With that one, I supposed that I was just very thirsty. I mean, despite our team having lost that evening, we did play a terribly fast-paced game. I managed to do better with the second beer, even though it seemed I had to wait four hours before ordering it.

To make a long story short, my experiment was, surprisingly, a total success, but at a price. I made it to my car feeling both physically and mentally drained. The time I took getting to know my team was spent in vain, for my concentration on my drinking had to be so focused that I had little fun and could only vaguely recollect any of the chatter that was going on around me. I was exhausted and dismayed that I had thrown away 89 days of sobriety and I hadn't bothered to get even a tiny bit drunk.

Yet, I also felt a stir of elation riding alongside an unfamiliar feeling of contented defeat. I realized that though my purpose was achieved this one time, in all likelihood it wouldn't be very long before I went back to how I typically drank.

I realized that even if I were able to sustain such a controlled drinking pattern for any length of time, in no form or fashion would I have what could be considered "normal" drinking habits. I mean, really, who but an alcoholic sets out to meticulously plot the course of his or her nightly drinking?

During the drive home, I let the surrender engulf me. There, in my car, I was finally able to take that First Step toward recovery. I conceded to my innermost self that I was powerless over alcohol and that my life and my drinking were unmanageable.

The next morning, I returned to my home group. They laughed merrily over my scheme and welcomed me back with commands that I stay. For nearly four years now, I've done just that, and not once have I again questioned whether or not I am an alcoholic.

NICKI J.
Los Angeles, California

CTALKING CDOG STORY
May 1962

M y wife, Mary, tells me that talking dog stories are silly and old-fashioned. She could be right.

You don't have to believe this. To me, today—dog fancier, breeder of prize-winning chihuahuas, treasurer of a thriving county bank—it never really happened. I prefer it that way. But there was this cold, moonless night in January:

Everything seemed betwixt and between. ... Between me and my house there were three hundred yards of unlighted road. And I was walking. Between me and my house was a low growl. The growl came from between two round spots of green light. The growl had a biting tone, and I could imagine there were teeth to match—big white teeth below and between the two round spots of green light, which, I could no longer doubt, were the eyes of a dog. A large dog.

The two round spots of green light, at large-dog-level, moved when I moved; when I tried to pass to the right they moved to the right, when I tried left they moved left. I gave up.

"Go on home, dog," I said, in what I thought was a firm tone.

"I hate drunks!" The answering resonance startled me.

Not so much because the dog had spoken. For some weeks, now, I had become accustomed to unlikely things trying to engage me in conversation. There was the shot glass which kept calling me "Shaky" until I switched to doubles. And the several bottles of beer at the Emerson Bar which persisted in falling over and saying, "Oops, I'm sorry," to the bartender. So the dog didn't startle me by talking. It was the tone. It lacked the amusing elfin quality of the whiskey glass and the beer bottles. It sounded too much like an angry dog and I wasn't in any shape to cope with angry dogs.

I said: "Let me pass, will you?"

"This is a purely personal opinion," opined the dog, "but I think drunks stink." He punctuated his accusation with a threatening snarl when I took a step forward. "To me, you drunks stink even when you don't smell, which is rarely. You drink and think like animals, and then you have the gall to call me a dog."

"Will you get out of my way and let me get home?"

"Why? So you can push people around because they're sober? Why don't you try pushing me around? You want to stagger in and start yammering at your wife and the kids just because ..."

"I don't want to yammer at anybody," I interrupted. "All I want to do is go home and get some sleep and go to church in the morning." I added senselessly and smugly: "You see, I'm not such an animal as you think I am."

"Church!" said the dog, "You know what your belief is?—spiritus frumenti! You know what your church is?—the First Church of John the Barleycorn! You know what you are?—you're a devout alcoholic!" He snickered. "Devout alcoholic."

I stepped forward, teetered on one foot, aimed a kick, and a yelp told me it had connected. I kicked again into thin air, slipped, sat down hard on gravel, and continued to sit there yelling: "You crazy dog! Dogs can't talk! D'you hear me, you crazy dog? Only crazy dogs can talk!"

The hands which lifted me to my feet were not gentle hands. They had a professional style in the way they held my right arm bent up behind me, with the palm of my hand to the small of my back. And my collar went tight from the thick fingers inserted in my neckband. I was spun around and I knew there was a car now in front of me, even though the headlights were out. I thought it might be a fancy taxi of some kind because of the revolving red and white light on top. Then the owner of the professional hands said: "Now stop yelling and get in the car." He kept his voice lowered, like an announcer at the symphony. The red and white light flickered on his badge.

"I want to go home," I said.

"Sure you do," the voice at my shoulder said. "And where's home?"

"Right back there—right up the road."

"What road are you talking about?" He opened the door of the darkened squad car. "Step up—that's the boy. Sit down."

"Frelinghuysen Road—isn't this Frelinghuysen Road?"

"If it is, it's ten miles from where it was this morning. This is Parkview, Doctor Parson's estate. And the doctor doesn't like you waking him up at two in the morning with all that yelling in his driveway."

At Cloverdale, Justice of the Peace Conley sat on the Sunday morning bench, immediately after church. He did this in order to clear the drunk tank and save the county the cost of Sunday dinners. Justice Conley adopted the sing-song of the absent clerk as he read to me across the bench.

"Robert Mead, violation of paragraph seven, section twelve sixty-three Civil Code, drunk, disorderly and disturbing the peace, how do you plead?"

I stared at him mutely because I was convinced that if I tried to say anything nothing would come out. I was shaky and I was Sahara-thirsty.

Justice Conley stared back. To him, I suppose, I was the sum essence of the eleven drunkards who had preceded me in this Sunday morning parade. And his stare was not mute. He said: "You didn't have any trouble with your loud mouth on Doctor Parson's estate last night—how do you plead?"

I stood and looked at him.

"Y'know," the Justice said, "this is a purely personal opinion, but I think drunks stink. To me, you drunks stink even when you don't smell, which is rarely. You drink and think like animals, and then you have the gall to expect me to temper justice with mercy!"

The words were the dog's words but the voice was the voice of justice.

I tried my own: "That's a misquote. He said, 'have the gall to call me a dog.'" It came out in a whisper. Something was terribly wrong with my vocal chords. But I managed to add in near-normal tones: "I just want to get home to my family."

"Why?" asked Justice Conley. "So you can push people around because they're sober? Why don't you try pushing me around? You want to stagger in and start yammering at your wife and the kids just because ..."

"Now you're saying exactly what he said," I interrupted. "Only that dog said 'gall to call me a dog,' instead of—"

"Bailiff, what is this man saying?" The Justice's inflammable temper was beginning to smolder.

"Sir, he said something about calling him a dog. Maybe he thinks like he feels. Maybe he thinks he's a dog."

"My opinion precisely," gritted Justice Conley. "Mead, what manner of animal are you, really? You told the officers you have a wife and children. You told them you were trying to get home so you could go to church this morning. You know what your belief is?—spiritus frumenti! What kind of a church finds spiritual kinship in a man of your caliber? WHAT church? What do you pretend to be? Answer me!"

As I said before, something had happened to my vocal chords. And my thinking. I wanted to bark and snarl and growl. But I responded to command.

The bailiff, leaning close to listen, heard me say: "I'm a devout alcoholic!" And then I barked. Not a loud bark, but not very friendly, either.

Well, thirty days will pass as all things pass, I suppose. And I ought to mention right here that I don't tell talking dog stories anymore. This is just—one for the road.

N. H.
Annapolis, Maryland

CHAPTER FIVE

"Well, what are you waiting for? Make him sober!"

ROUNDING UP
THE USUAL SUSPECTS
Twelfth-Step calls that didn't quite go as expected

I n "I Knocked on the Wrong Door," an AA on a Twelfth-Step call wonders why the prospect doesn't remember asking the hospital chaplain to call AA for him. But the man, obviously a heavy drinker, comes to a meeting with the member anyway. Turns out it was the wrong man—but the "wrong man" likes what he hears and decides to give AA a shot. In "Sponsoring the Ala-Tot," the author compares his newborn son's "total self-absorption" and "complete lack of gratitude" to some behaviors he's witnessed in AA "babies." AAs in this chapter talk about the unusual Twelfth-Step work they've done over the years.

I KNOCKED ON THE WRONG DOOR

February 1961

In October 1958 some of us helped start a group in the VA Hospital in our city and have worked actively at it since. We have received a lot of cooperation from the staff and especially from the Protestant chaplain, who is quite a dedicated man.

About three weeks ago the chaplain called me and said there was a patient on the seventh floor of the hospital who had told him he would like to talk to someone from Alcoholics Anonymous about his drinking. The chaplain couldn't remember the man's full name but said that his last name was Johnson and to go on up to that floor and the ward attendant would point him out to me. Since I was pretty much occupied with some other AA work right then and couldn't make the call myself, I called our clubhouse and turned it over to them. Usually that is all that is necessary and the call is promptly made.

On VA Hospital meeting night, a couple of days later, I went up to see Johnson and discovered that he had checked out of the hospital the day before. I didn't think too much more about it, but a week later discovered that due to a misunderstanding the call from the club had not been made and no one had contacted Johnson. This is a mistake that is sometimes made and I suppose we just goofed.

The following week, while talking with the chaplain at the hospital I told him we had missed his man, how it happened and apologized. He then called the administrative office and gave me Johnson's full name and address. Since he lived here in our city I felt that we might hear from him again.

Back in my office I got to thinking about Johnson and felt that this man just might be somewhere right that minute probably cussing AA as a whole because he had asked for help and we hadn't come, so I got in my car and drove to his home to explain to him. The shades were drawn and the air-conditioner was running full blast, but no one answered my knock on the door. Now, this is familiar to some of us and so I just kept pounding on his door. Finally the door opened and a man stood in front of me, clad only in his britches, barely able to stand. He asked me in and I told him who I was and that I had come from AA in response to his conversation with the chaplain. He seemed rather vague on that point and kept insisting he couldn't remember talking to the chaplain about it. He was talking of suicide and was crying, laughing, heaving, and in fact just pretty damned sick. He finally said he might want to try to get sober and agreed to go to the clubhouse with me. We kept him in the club about two hours and he'd had enough. He said he wanted to leave, so I took him to the northern part of our city to a place where his girlfriend worked and let him out. I had given him a "Way of Life" pamphlet with my name and phone number on it. The last I saw of him he was weaving down the street with that little blue book sticking out of his hip pocket.

The next day I called the chaplain to tell him what happened to his man and he quickly informed me that he was indeed sorry but he had made a mistake in names and that the man he'd talked to was named Jones instead of Johnson. He said he knew Johnson but that both he and Johnson's doctor thought that AA, or anybody else, was wasting their time trying to talk to him. I suppose I agreed with him and went on about my business.

I quickly was given the name "wrong man Bill," and everybody I knew had a pretty good laugh. Well, I suppose it was kind of funny—but there is a sequel.

A week ago the phone at the clubhouse rang about ten o'clock in the morning—yes, it was my friend Johnson. He wanted help. When we went to get him he'd gone without a drink for several hours, trying to get up guts to call us, and he acted as though he really wanted what AA has to offer. He was taken to our Twelfth Step House where he stayed five days. He left there this morning, sober, bright-eyed, looking for a job, and apparently literally "risen from the dead." He had been drunk continually since 1953 and hadn't worked a day during that time. His eyes were shining this morning when he left and he looked like a different man. You know the change that took place because you've seen it yourselves.

Now, if he's an alcoholic, we all know he could get drunk again tomorrow, but somehow I'm going to believe that this Higher Power we talk about so much was working a little overtime last week, and that whether my boy stays sober or not, I stood in the very presence of God that day when Johnson opened the door for me, tears in his eyes, and grabbed me around the neck and said he wanted to try.

B. C.
Oklahoma City, Oklahoma

YOU TAKE HIM
June 1999

It was a Sunday night just before the start of the 7:30 meeting, a podium discussion meeting, which I attended on a regular basis. I was standing outside when a car pulled up and a woman got out who appeared to be in her middle thirties, nicely dressed and with a stern look. She went over to the passenger's side and opened the car door. She reached inside, grabbed a wet drunk, and pulled him out. He could hardly walk. All she said was, "I don't want him anymore. You take him."

Well, I went into the meeting and got a friend of mine to help me with this drunk outside. The man was really bombed, slurring his words, reeking of booze, and was dirty and unkempt. We got him into my friend's truck and took him to my friend's home. We sat in the living room, wondering what to do with this guy. The drunk seemed to want to go to a hospital and be admitted to its alcoholic ward. We both agreed that he had probably done this many times before.

So off to the hospital we went, about an hour's drive, and on the way this guy kept wanting to kiss us. His breath was terrible. A drunk in his cups is not a pretty sight or smell. We got to the hospital and waited a long time to get him admitted. It was a county hospital in a large city with so many people in the waiting room we thought he would never get in. But he did. While the doctor was reviewing his case, we went outside for some fresh night air. Actually it was almost midnight. About twenty minutes went by and we went back in to find out what the doctor was going to do with him. We couldn't find the guy. He wasn't in the observation room and the nurse didn't know his whereabouts. We asked around, and a fellow patient said he'd taken off out the exit door real fast. Our Twelfth-Step candidate was gone, gone, gone, gone. So we headed home and stopped for some breakfast. It was a long night, but we had enjoyed ourselves. We finished our meal and got home into bed around three A.M.

Neither of us heard from this drunk, nor did we see him at any meetings. I ran into the woman who had dropped him off, and she told me that he'd moved to the East Coast and was really drinking there. He had been her boyfriend and had moved back to her hometown on the East Coast where her folks knew him.

About five years passed. One day I got a message on my answering machine thanking me for my help that night. This fellow had been sober in AA for two years. I got the message on Christmas Day—what a present!

RON N.
Oakhurst, California

SPONSORING THE ALA-TOT
December 1962

One July morning in 1961 my wife awoke early and complained of severe abdominal pains. I rushed her to the hospital, where she suddenly disappeared down an antiseptic corridor while a bossy old woman in a starched uniform ordered me into a waiting room. For two hours I read an upside-down copy of a year-old magazine and carried on a jerky conversation with a young man who stood with one foot on a radiator and scowled out the window. He was much younger than I, yet it was his third experience of this sort. I could not bring myself to admit that it was my first time, even though I was almost thirty-six.

I had begun to resent the fertile young man's superior ways very much when I saw my wife being wheeled on a table past the open door of the waiting room. She was lying on her stomach, a feat she hadn't performed now in many months. The bossy old woman followed close behind and growled that I could come to see my wife in a few minutes, but the visit would have to be necessarily short so as to avoid contamination of her room. And so it was, that ten minutes later I was stand-

---

HAM ON WRY:

TWO AAs WERE MAKING A TWELFTH STEP CALL. DURING THE PROCEEDINGS, THE ACTIVE ALCOHOLIC ASKED ONE OF THEM HOW LONG HE HAD BEEN A MEMBER OF THE FELLOWSHIP? "TEN YEARS," WAS THE REPLY. HE NODDED, THEN PUT THE QUESTION TO THE SECOND MAN, WHO ANSWERED, "FIVE WEEKS." THE SUFFERING ALCOHOLIC STARED. "FIVE WEEKS!" HE EXCLAIMED. "HOW IN HELL DID YOU DO IT?!"

– ANONYMOUS, JANUARY 1964

ing close to my wife's bed when our newborn son, Wayne William, was brought in for an introduction.

And in this moment I was smitten by a tidal wave of fear. Here was I, the longtime AA, the confirmed bachelor, the sometime recluse, responsible for a creature who was apparently illiterate and incapable of supporting himself. He couldn't walk, speak, distinguish objects, or even feed himself. And he wasn't at all pretty. His head was shaped like an underfed gourd and his face had an angry, squinched-together look. I was quite certain that he was just a miniature King Kong without hair.

The nurse was babbling on excitedly about what a lovely baby he was, but I dismissed her chatter as part of the hypocritical sales talk the hospital professionals use. After all, if they didn't do some kind of a selling job, you'd be inclined to leave the babies there or have them shipped off to the zoo. I felt like saying, "Okay, lay off, lady." But I didn't want to hurt the gushy old soul's feelings, and I also perceived that the sales talk had apparently brainwashed my wife, because she obviously didn't notice the gourd-shaped head and the wrinkled face. Then I remember that my wife probably hadn't ever heard of King Kong, either!

Five days later, in a gesture that still strikes me as being brutal and sadistic, the hospital abruptly stopped caring for my wife and Wayne William, and I found myself alone with them at the front entrance, nervously preparing for the drive home. By now the gourd-shaped head had started to turn into the more acceptable outlines of a cantaloupe, and his face seemed less wrinkled and not quite so angry. I scrutinized him carefully and decided he was definitely less repulsive than he had been at our first meeting. I started the car and drove home at two miles an hour.

For the next two weeks I endured the unendurable. Shrill screams catapulted me from the bed at 2:00 a.m. I stepped on mushy diapers that had been left lying around. I spent most of my spare time on errands, for this new creature required an incredible amount of maintenance equipment. Bills began to pour in. I was trapped, helpless, feeling almost drowned in responsibility.

As it always does, the AA philosophy came galloping to the rescue with a program of action for the care of babies. Good old AA had saved my life more than ten years before, and had somehow always been flexible enough—versatile enough—to show me ways out of other life problems. It had taught me how to co-exist with despotic employers. It had schooled me in the art of getting along with impossible people. It had even shown me that one of those impossible persons with whom I hadn't been at all on good terms was myself, and before many months the magic AA program had healed that troubled relationship. Now what did it have to teach me about getting along with this difficult newcomer, this source of midnight disturbances and treacherous diapers?

It had quite a bit to teach me. For one thing, as an AA member I had always called new members by the customary term "babies." For another, I had long recognized that alcoholics were emotionally immature persons, which by inference means that in some respects they still belonged in the cradle. Finally, I have believed that the AA program is an infallible guide to success in human relationships, and especially in family relationships. Isn't fatherhood actually a form of sponsorship? Doesn't one have the task of taking a helpless individual by the hand and helping him to grow to independence? True, AA sponsorship is brief, casual and relatively uncomplicated, while fatherhood is a lifetime responsibility, but both should have the goal of helping persons to achieve freedom, usefulness and some degree of blessedness. The wise sponsor will even want to see his "baby" eventually surpass him in these things.

Now I'll admit that in the beginning Wayne William—my Anonymous Ala-Tot—showed little promise. A listing of some of his chief traits shows how similar he was to many of the "babies" who come into AA:

TOTAL SELF-ABSORPTION: Seemed aware only of himself and his immediate needs.

INABILITY TO FEED SELF: Was unable to raise food and drink to his own lips.

COMPLETE LACK OF GRATITUDE: Took what he wanted when he wanted it, without so much as a single grateful acknowledgment.

LACK OF CONSIDERATION FOR OTHERS: Emitted loud noises even

though others were trying desperately to sleep.

UTTER LACK OF MODESTY: Showed total disregard for his state of absolute nudity even in the presence of several female visitors.

ATROCIOUS MANNERS: Made slurping sounds while taking nourishment and belched loudly upon finishing.

As Wayne William's sponsor, I perceived that these traits were charming and lovable in babies, but were terrible liabilities in the adult world. It is too early to tell, but I cannot help but feel that it is far easier to guide a young child into the good life than it is a sick adult in whom selfishness and pride have become deeply imbedded. So far AA has been largely a remedial program, correcting attitudes of mind and spirit that never should have been twisted in the first place. Won't its principles have a far greater effect on the tender child who never has been warped and twisted by cruelty, neglect, lovelessness and all the other forces of hate? I believe that they will.

Right from the beginning, though, I began going against the advice of almost everybody who had ever "raised" babies. Some of them told me that I didn't know anything about "raising" children, but I hardly listened to what they had to say, for I had seen some of their babies grow into impudent little brats with severe emotional problems. And I don't think my wife and I even cared for the word "raise"; one "raises" rabbits, chickens and cabbages, but children ought to be in another category. They deserve much more than mere "raising"; they deserve sponsorship. And I had far more experience at sponsorship than any of the old wives who clucked their tongues at the way we dealt with Wayne William.

For example, I discovered in his first few days at home that he would stop crying if we would feed him, rock his bassinet, or pick him up and carry him around the room. I reasoned that he cried because he was pained, hungry, uncomfortable, or frightened. His crying was the only way he had of telling us this, so immediately our policy was established: If he cries, pick him up.

I was amazed by the number of people who warned me that I was "spoiling" our baby. Some even suggested that he was manipulating us, and had "got the best" of us. I didn't listen very closely to their advice, for sometimes good AA sponsorship requires that we place ourselves in a position to be "manipulated" and "used" by unscrupulous or misguided people who don't really want what our program has to offer. But I was certain that an infant child is not unscrupulous or misguided, and cannot really have any cunning knowledge that he is "using" somebody. So we continued to pick him up, and after a few months he seemed to demand it less and less. Now he rarely cries. People remark that he is such a happy baby, but I wonder if he would be so if we had left him to scream away his terrors in the loneliness of a locked room.

Another of our policies, or beliefs, was that a baby has all the rights and privileges due any human being, and must be treated with respect. In my years of bachelorhood I had scowled ferociously while young parents humiliated their children in public or tended to neglect them. I had often suspected that these same parents had been treated in a similar way when they were children, as had I, but this was at best a very shabby reason for passing the same cruelty on to one's own children. Good sponsorship must include a genuine respect for the baby and a willingness to spend some time with him.

So, soon after we brought him home from the hospital, I began to take Wayne William for long walks in his stroller, often without my wife. I noticed that other men looked at me rather peculiarly, and I realized that in our society it is usually women who take the baby for walks. The more I thought about it, the more I realized that many men actually spend very little time with their children. So much of our AA sponsorship has a threadbare quality because we haven't as yet learned how to love the helpless and sometimes disagreeable people who come to us. We sponsor them mechanically, without really putting much of ourselves into it. The AA member who has a genuine love of others rises above this, and provides a far greater sponsorship than is otherwise possible. And this has its effect on the "baby."

It's a poor sponsorship that doesn't have a wondrous effect on the sponsor too, and I can truthfully say that sponsoring the baby has done me more good than almost any previous experience. By becoming a father myself, I've had a better understanding of the role of God as Father of Man. I tell myself that if God loves us even as much as I love my little boy, then all is going to be well with the world. And I have felt a lessening of self-concern, more personal fulfillment, and a keener understanding of the adult world around me. I've even felt a little closer to AA, which of course made my sponsorship of the Anonymous Ala-Tot possible in the first place.

M.D.B.
Michigan

HEARD IN THE BLIZZARD
September 1948

C hicago legends include the story about the two AAs there who worked on morning newspapers and consequently got quite a few early morning Twelfth Step calls.

On this particular midnight, one winter several years ago, a blizzard was blowing right off Lake Michigan. The two were responding to a call for help from way out on the edge of the city. They were wading through the snow, battling a sharp wind and wondering aloud how they ever got into this AA business anyway.

Finally, one said: "Yeah, this is tough all right. But do you remember where we were a year ago tonight?"

The other, not to be mollified, snapped back: "No I don't, but I'll bet we were somewhere drunk and minding our own business!"

ANONYMOUS
Chicago, Illinois

(THE PARLOR PROSPECT
July 1998

I t was after midnight when the middle-aged lady opened the door and invited George and me into her well-kept parlor. She didn't look like a person who had just phoned AA for help. At first we thought someone else in the house might have the alcohol problem but as it turned out, she was our pigeon.

George and I each shared a little of our stories. She listened politely and seemed to identify. She expressed none of the usual hostility and in fact, shared her own story eagerly, all the while serving us coffee in fine china. Her drinking didn't seem all that bad to us. She was a school librarian, so we didn't expect a background of booze like a stevedore's or a salesman's. Time to chalk up another successful Twelfth-Step call ... or so we thought.

After an hour or two, the woman agreed that AA was her answer and looked forward to attending a meeting with us that night. Then she said, "I do have one concern. I belong to a church where wine is part of the communion service. You've told me that AAs don't drink anything, so I wonder, how can I join your group and remain a member of my church?"

She was in luck. George and I were both recent graduates of a Jesuit university where courses in philosophy and theology had prepared us for just such a moment. We took turns quoting Augustine, Aquinas, and Pius in an earnest if misguided attempt to ease this lady's moral burden. She knew we could tell a psalm from a syllogism and was obviously impressed. (It didn't occur to George or me that no intellectual expertise had ever prevented John Barleycorn from having his way with either of us.)

It was late and we all had to go to work in a few hours. We started to leave with a firm resolve to continue our discourse that evening. Suddenly, George, in a rare moment of clarity asked, "This is a one-day-at-a-time program. Are you planning to take communion this morning?"

"Oh no," she replied. "I haven't been to church in years!"

To my knowledge, this lady has yet to attend an AA meeting. I don't know if she was an alcoholic or simply a lonely lady who was a little mixed-up. But on the way to our meeting that night, back in the early 1960s, George and I spent a lot of time laughing at ourselves. We had learned a valuable lesson: to take this program seriously but never ourselves!

JIM M.
Escondido, California

⸀BLACKBIRDS HELPED CONVINCE⸲ CUSTOMER
August 1947

About five years ago, when I thought AA could be sold to people who didn't want it, I journeyed some 75 miles each way to see a chap who was confined in my old alma mater where I had spent some nine weeks—and learned nothing about alcoholism nor about myself as an alcoholic. I would see that this didn't happen to him, by golly! No, sir! I would spread the glad tidings of great joy and he would come home and never take another drink as long as he lived. This fellow was a smart cookie—a super C.P.A., and working for an important outfit. He couldn't miss, I said to myself. What if gasoline and tires are rationed? Get yourself up there. Yes, sir! That's what I said and what I did. Well naturally, he thought it was swell, but of course, it didn't apply to him, so five years slipped by until the afternoon that he called me and asked for help.

The five years had not used him very kindly, and as he sat on the sofa in my living room, shaking to pieces, he presented rather a sorry picture. I immediately asked him how he was, and he said, "Fine" and

I countered quickly with, "You don't look it," so we got down to cases. We talked at length. (Anyone reading this who has not seen "The Lost Weekend" can just stop here and read something interesting. I should have warned you to start with.) As we talked I heard a slight rustling in my fireplace, to which I paid no attention. We talked on. He thought he might be losing his mind, maybe. More rustling in the fireplace. Maybe he was going to have DTs, he thought. He felt like he was going to jump out of his skin, he said. About that time—whoosh! Out of that fireplace flew a blackbird that promptly began to fly around my living room. Behind him and hard on his heels came another! Behind him came another—and another—and another, until six of those things were circling around like mad!

He took one look and froze solid with his hands over his eyes to blot out this unreality. Occasionally he would peek out, but it was still going on. I guess he wondered why I was killing myself laughing. He hadn't seen the picture. It wasn't funny to him, not by a long shot. Well, I caught them all, four in the living room and two in the pantry. Alone and unaided I caught them. He was still unable to move. "What a thing to do to a drunk!" he said. I think he still thinks I planned it. One of the boys said he thought the Man Upstairs planned it. Anyway, it looks like we have a pretty good man now.

J. C. H.
Ferguson, Missouri

WHO? ME?
September 1949

Two of us were answering a Twelfth Step call. We pushed the bell and the door opened to reveal a sorry-looking man peering at us through red-rimmed, bloodshot eyes. He was extremely nervous, but very polite. We said we were from AA and he invited us in, but the perspiration was dripping off him even though it was a cool evening. We figured this lad was ready to settle for almost anything.

Imagine our surprise when, as soon as we found chairs in the living room, our hangdog host said, "Of course, you know, I didn't call AA for myself!" (Heavens, no!) "It's about my ... er ... my ... uncle!" Joe and I looked at each other but said, "Of course, of course ... your uncle!"

So for two hours we sat there talking about "poor Uncle Louie." During that time our host excused himself three times, went to the back of the house, and returned smelling to high heaven of whiskey and coffee grounds. Poor "Uncle Louie"!

As we were leaving, my pal Joey turned to our new friend and said he'd heard a pretty good story that afternoon.

"Seems this guy showed up at a psychiatrist's office," said Joe. "He had two strips of bacon, very crisp, sticking out from under his hat. One on each side, like elaborate sideburns. As he sat down alongside the doctor's desk he removed his hat and there, in the exact center of his head, was a beautiful fried egg. The psychiatrist pretended he didn't notice and asked, 'What can I do for you?' Whereupon the big egg-and-bacon man said, 'Oh no, Doctor, not me! I came to talk about my brother!'

Then Joe and I said, "Good night!"

ANONYMOUS

CHAPTER SIX

"Harry, do you have anything to add to the discussion?"

LIVE AND LEARN

Stuff my sponsor says, and other lessons from meetings and life

"Don't drink and go to meetings." "Keep It Simple" (with or without the "Stupid"). "First Things First." Those obvious pieces of advice are accessible to new and old AAs, and are typically on display in meeting rooms. They work very well. But there are always nuggets of wisdom not found in the literature or in the slogans, such as "When I was drinking, I was afraid I was not achieving my potential. Now that I'm sober, I worry that maybe I am," shared in the story "Meetings, Meetings, Meetings." Then there is the declaration from a sponsor retold in a letter to Grapevine: "Everybody loves me." When asked how he could claim this, he replies, "No one has told me that they don't love me." Here, some AAs share about the moments of inspiration and clarity that helped them grow.

IT'S A MĪRACLE͜ɔ!

September 2010

"You just can't make this (stuff) up." That was printed on a business card, with a picture of Snoopy dressed as a sleuth, that was handed to me recently by an old man in my sunrise meeting, and it aptly articulates the reason I am writing this story. Because no matter what I come up with for a storyline, how amazingly developed the characters are, or what aha! moments they may stumble upon, nothing can come close to real life. Turns out, God's a better storyteller than I am.

I was just over 30 when I finally decided to take responsibility for my life. After a particularly gruesome scene the night before, my boyfriend and I admitted to ourselves and to each other that the party was over—it was time to stop drinking.

I remember our first AA meeting vividly. It was Friday night at about 8:00 P.M., a time when ordinarily we would have been running around Manhattan, wasted after a happy hour and wondering where we were going to go next. Instead, we were walking around Park Slope in Brooklyn, trying to get through the evening with as little resentment as possible. From inside a church, we heard thunderous applause. My boyfriend looked at me, relieved for a diversion from our bored self-pity and said, "Must be a free concert. C'mon, let's check it out." And so we stepped through the doors—right into an AA anniversary meeting.

I wasn't completely sure I was an alcoholic at that point, but I was willing to learn more, and that was enough. The next meeting I went to, I went to alone.

As I was walking I started talking to God. Not out loud, but in my head. I was bargaining, questioning and testing. The serendipitous experience of my first AA meeting didn't convince me. I needed a sign of some sort that I was on the right path by going to AA. As soon as I finished the thought, my eye caught sight of a dollar bill on the ground. Nice work, God, I thought as I picked it up. Not bad. But maybe you could show me something else? Something more obvious?

Just then I heard a woman shriek from across the street. "It's a miracle!" she exclaimed. Whoa! Yes, that's what I'm talking about, God! Curious, I walked toward her. She had her back to me. I tapped her shoulder and asked what she meant, as she seemed to be talking to herself about miracles. She smiled happily at me. "It's my puppy," she said, holding a little black fur ball for me to see. "He finally did it! He waited to go to the bathroom outside!"

"Oh," I said. I guess I must have looked sad or disappointed, because suddenly her eyes turned soft and she put her hand on my shoulder.

"I think the place you're looking for is on the corner across the street." I followed her gaze and saw a tall cathedral with people standing outside smoking.

"I think you're right," I said.

"And it is a miracle," she said.

I smiled and said, "I hope so."

And it was.

MOIRA L.
Norwalk, Connecticut

LONG LIVE THE WIMP
November 2007

I've read recently that alcoholics who can't or won't stop drinking should be schooled in practices that reduce the harm they may cause, such as giving their car keys to a friend before drinking.

It's a good idea, and I'd be happy to hold car keys for anybody who plans to get drunk. But instead, I prefer to advocate the harm avoidance I've found in the AA program. Rather than reduce harm, I want to avoid it—completely if possible.

I learned about avoiding harm 21 years ago, after taking a routine psychology test. The psychologist told me that I had a very high level of harm avoidance, a new term for me. He said I wasn't the kind of a guy who would be a skydiver or a motorcycle racer, to say nothing of other hazardous pursuits. This diagnosis left me feeling glum and unmanly. In my fantasies, I was John Wayne charging an enemy-held beach or Gary Cooper shooting it out with the bad guys in "High Noon." Now it was obvious that I would never be in that league. As I told a friend, "I got to be 60 years old only to learn that I'm a wimp."

My friend saw it differently. "Maybe that's how you got to be 60 years old!" he said.

That was some consolation. It helped even more when I could reflect that a strong desire to avoid harm may have helped keep me in AA for so many years. When drinking, I had sometimes taken daredevil actions that made me shudder after I sobered up.

Such actions go along with drinking, but, in sobriety, I have always displayed caution and prudence. I can't even stand to look at skydivers performing, and I wouldn't even be a spectator at a motorcycle race, let alone a participant. (After all, motorcycles can get out of control and come over the fence at you!)

So, staying completely sober also meant avoiding the terrible risks that seemed to go along with drinking. One example: It's been more than 60 years since I tried to punch out a cop, and I hope to go another 50 years without doing it.

I'm now 82 and have added another 21 years to the sobriety I had when I first learned I was a wimp who avoided harm. I'll still try to reduce the harm for anyone still drinking, even though it's risky to take car keys away from a drunk. But I would also ask, "Why risk any harm at all if it can be avoided by staying sober?"

Fortunately, though outed as a wimp, I can still keep my fantasies. That's because I have my own copy of "High Noon."

MEL B.
Toledo, Ohio

MEETINGS, MEETINGS, MEETINGS

October 1981

S.H. from Hilton Head Island, South Carolina, writes about a guest at a local hotel who wanted to attend a meeting. He got the AA number from the bulletin board and called to find out about times and places.

A new girl was working the answering service, and after referring to the information she'd been given about AA meetings, came back with this reply: "I'm sorry, sir. The meeting that's usually held at the Presbyterian church has been closed, but the one Sunday night at the Episcopal church will be open."

Fortunately, the visitor had been a member long enough to understand and appreciate the girl's confusion, was able to set her straight on open and closed meetings, and appeared at the meeting that night with the amusing story that according to the answering service, it was closed.

And T. M. from Grand Rapids, Michigan, collected wisdom from local meetings:

"When I was drinking, I was afraid I was not achieving my potential. Now that I'm sober, I worry that maybe I am."

"One reason I don't like to talk about what I did when I was drunk is that I don't like to repeat hearsay."

"The worst thing about my problems is that they are mine."

"More and more, I am grateful for the things I used to be proud of."

"The best way to appreciate AA is the same way you appreciate a stained-glass window: Look at it from the inside."

COMING ABOUT
March 2003

The water glittered in the sun like a million antique mirrors. My friend Harry and I skimmed the surface, delighting in the spray of brine, the sweep of breeze. We were sailing Harry's Sunfish in the Gulf of California, and it was my first time so far from shore. In spite of the beauty of the moment, I began to fear capsizing. After all, the boat was quite small and the bay was as big as the sea. We were no more than specks. The more I thought about it, the more I worried. The shore became a thin suggestion of a line. I asked, in what I hoped sounded like a nonchalant tone (but Harry knows me well), "What would happen if we did lose control and fall in?" Harry reassured me, saying there was nothing at all to worry about. If he felt he was losing control, he demonstrated, he would simply let go. And the moment he did that, over we went! The warm water embraced us, and we bobbed there, laughing. It was a real lesson in letting go and turning it over!

DIANA S.
Tucson, Arizona

LIFE IN THE EXPRESS LANE
May 2009

When you are in a 10-items-or-less line in a supermarket checkout, and the person in front of you has more than 10 items and that no longer bothers you, that's acceptance. If you no longer count the number of items the person in front of you is buying, that's serenity.

PAUL K.
Beverly, Massachusetts

EVERYBODY LOVES ME
(from Dear Grapevine)
September 2006

The letter "Little Measures" in the June 2006 issue made me reflect on something that my sponsor helped me to learn: He said, "Everybody loves me." When I finished laughing—which was right after I realized that he wasn't laughing—I asked him how he could make such a statement.

He replied, "No one has told me that they don't love me."

I was new and I thought this was a touch on the odd side, but it stuck in my mind. I wanted what my sponsor had—he was happy, joyous, and free. He told me that I could have what he had if I did what he did to get it. So I decided that everybody loved me, too.

The transformation was amazing. Since everybody loved me, I treated them all better. Boss, coworkers, clerks, cashiers, bus drivers, fellow AAs, anyone—I treated them with love. They treated me better in return, and I know it made me feel better.

Today, I know that everybody loves me, and I base it on the fact that no one has told me that they don't.

MARK E.
Lansing, Michigan

LESSON OF THE DAY
(from Dear Grapevine)
March 2010

My Higher Power often reminds me gently and with humor when I am straying from the path, and speaks to me through other people.

On the first day back to school in the New Year, I was engaged in an after-school tutoring session with a 13-year-old student. When I asked how his first day went, he sadly lamented how quickly the two-week holiday had transpired. I attempted to cheer him up by explaining that if two weeks whizzed by that quickly, the 10 weeks until the March break would sail by. My student instantly grinned, and added, "Before we know it, summer vacation will be here!"

I felt I'd cheered him up. Then his face darkened and he muttered, "Holy crow, before I know it, I'll be dead!" I am happy to say that we both launched into a delightful two-hour session of learning and fun. It reminded me how good life is in sobriety, one day at a time.

VICTORIA M.
Toronto, Ontario

SHORT AND SWEET *(from Dear Grapevine)*
December 2009

T he author of "To Make a Long Story Short," (September 2009) prefers shorter stories. Do you suppose this life story (mine) would be a suitable example?

"Puny, clumsy and inept, I was thrust terrified into the swift traffic of life's main drag. I stumbled, mumbled and fumbled my way through the rigors of my generation, avoiding most challenges and failing nearly all the rest. Alcohol and phenobarbital became my refuge and my sanctuary—and my Judas. Now, in my 46th year of AA sobriety, with gratitude to prayer and Providence, I cultivate my thoughts and survey my convictions with some measure of satisfaction, bask in the doting attention of my life's companion and our gaggle of admiring descendants, and raise as much Cain as I can with shifty-eyed politicians."

RAY C.
Mill Valley, California

A RIBBITING IMAGE *(from Dear Grapevine)*
December 2008

T he picture of the frog ("Half-Measured," August 2008) illustrated what Lowell B., who got sober in 1967, once told me. Early in my sobriety, I was in agony over something now long forgotten.

I asked Lowell, "What do you do in times like this?" He advised, "You hang on!" I whined, "What good will that do?" He said, "If nothing else, it will give you one hell of a grip!"

At the time, it was the dumbest thing I'd ever heard an educated man say, but it's been with me every day for more than 35 years.

Your picture carried me happily back to that day in Lowell's office.

JIM W.
Redington Beach, Florida

POOR KEN *(from Dear Grapevine)*
August 1986

Recently I was asked to chair a noon discussion meeting. I accepted despite some uncomfortable cold symptoms which would have made it easier to remain in the back row and rest my vocal cords. When I started to qualify I referred to my miserable physical state as an explanation for keeping my remarks brief. There was an immediate response of: "Oh, poor Ken." Inspired by this unexpected source of sympathy, I raised my arms like an orchestra conductor and asked to hear those treasured words again. On my signal I received a tumultuous "Oh, poor Ken!" I loved it and so did the participants. It demonstrated how easily we can indulge in self-pity and how effectively our AA friends can snap us out of it with good humor.

K. E.
Rumford, Rhode Island

HEARD AT MEETINGS:
"ALCOHOLICS ARE THE ONLY PEOPLE IN THE WORLD WHO WANT A PULITZER PRIZE FOR WRITING A CHECK!"
– ED L., WRIGHTWOOD, CALIFORNIA, NOVEMBER 2008

CHAPTER SEVEN

NOVEMBER 1963

*". . . and he didn't drop the turkey or spill the gravy and everybody
was happy! It was the best Thanksgiving we ever had!"*

NOT-SO-SILENT NIGHTS

Holiday adventures and disasters before and after getting sober

Holidays can be times of great joy, with family and friends
gathered around and good food (without booze). For those
in a particular faith, some holidays hold great meaning. But
for AAs without family and friends, these annual events can be rough.
In "The Christmas Fighters," one former Scrooge* decides to share
Christmas morning with several others who had considered skipping
it altogether and realizes, "There seems to me now no more point to
being joyless on December 25th than to wake up and deliberately
encourage a bad humor on any other day of the year." In "Holidays,
Shmolidays," a recovering curmudgeon writes about Thanksgiving:
"Today I choose to be thankful to have a mostly serene sobriety. ...
Every day truly is a holiday, if you have the right spiritual awareness."
The stories in the following pages talk about celebrating and surviv-
ing the holidays, both before and after putting down the drink.

─────────────────

(*) Character from a Dickens story

⌃THE CHRISTMẤS FIGHTER⌄S
December 1963

❝ T he thing I'm really dreading," said Recently Divorced, "is Christmas."
"Dreading Christmas?" asked Recently Sober. "What about New Year's Eve?"

Since this conversation took place in August, one might seriously wonder if it weren't a slight case of misplaced anxiety. But to the really dedicated Christmas Fighter, time is not an object. I know. I used to be one.

True, I didn't usually start fulminating until the Monday after Thanksgiving when the turkey advertisements came down and the Santa Clauses went up all over New York City. And the wreaths. And the bells. And the trees. Off with the yellow and brown, on with the red and green. And in my case, up the rebels. "It's so commercial," I would begin. "Disgusting and commercial!" There usually was a commercial, piping cheerily and obligingly from a radio or TV set in the background, "X number of shopping days until Christmas," to lend support to my words. "Listen to that," I would say. "Just listen."

Of course I wasn't the only one. There were plenty of voices raised in protest, and still are. "How commercial!" they cry up and down the land as they pore over the catalogues to decide what to buy, and thumb through the ads to decide what to ask for, or get trampled into insensibility in the merry free-for-all that is known as Christmas Shopping.

Perhaps there are some purists who eschew all that, ask not and give not and let December 25th go by. (I heard of a lady, not quite a purist, who shopped and sent her presents in July with a "Do not open until Christmas" written firmly on the outside so she could avoid her holiday hysteria.)

But most Christmas Fighters aren't that well-organized. My own rebellion was a sort of over-all dragging of the feet, shopping too late rather than too early, thus missing the worst of the rush, but also missing the best of the things I wanted to buy. Not wrapping anything until I was enroute in a taxicab, if I could get a taxicab, and then letting it all go with some creased paper and a bit of tape. Complaining to some members of the family about having to cope with other members of the family. Being late for Christmas dinner, slow to open my presents and dreading the moment when others opened the haphazard ones I gave. (And yet once upon a time, as a child, I had made my presents by hand, wrapped them elaborately, and stayed awake all night. What had happened, that now made it all so gray?)

I couldn't put it all down to my drinking days, although the last holiday before I came into AA was certainly the original gray Christmas. My hands shook so I could not open the mound of packages prepared for me; Christmas dinner was an endless ordeal. The next year, very new in AA, I remember hearing that the holidays were a tricky time for us, which is perhaps true in the beginning, laden as they are with old associations, obligations or, perhaps, new loneliness. So I armed myself for the "tricky time," advanced toward it with all my AA reinforcements, phone numbers, and slogans, which was fine then and a good idea. But the militant mood persisted in the intervening years.

And then, suddenly, everything changed. The family that had seemed as immovable as the rock of Manhattan itself dispersed in one short year. One branch went to Hawaii, another to Vermont, a third just decided to get out of town for the holidays. Christmas became a blank, just another twenty-four hours I could do with as I wished. Go to friends, not go to friends, go to church, go to the movies—it was up to me. I began to heave a sigh of relief, but it turned into a sigh that was oddly bereft; and then I started to behave in a most peculiar way. It was not planned, or thought out, or deliberate. It was instinct, impulse, spontaneity revived; a motor that had been dormant since childhood turned over and began to cough a little, chug once or twice, and finally catch on. A hum filled a silent space.

The first sign of it came about two weeks before C-Day. I was sitting in my apartment with an AA friend and I said: "Listen, I haven't had a Christmas tree for ages. Let's go and get one." We rushed out and picked and chose and haggled with the sidewalk "tree people," and then we picked and chose and haggled some more over ornaments, and whether snow or no snow would be better, and whether it would be more fun with lights. Perhaps that's the key word: fun. It might have been for fun, that tree. Anyhow we got our selections back to the apartment and invited some neighbors over, and then another AA friend, and soon the place was full of people deciding first that the star at the top was boring, then deciding it wasn't.

Once the tree was up in all its glory, another idea developed. I had two AA friends whose reservations about the holidays were as tried and true as my own, confirmed Christmas Fighters of the old school. One had a Family Affair to face up to in the afternoon; the other, as a matter of conviction and resolve, had Nothing To Do. I called them both. "I know how Against Everything we all are," I started out, "and how we hate the phony sentimentality and all, but I've got a plan. Maybe if just the three of us did something on Christmas Day, it would be fun. How about breakfast at my place?" "Perfect," said Family Affair. "It'll give me the strength to face the rest of it." Nothing To Do was more cautious: "Well," he said, "I guess it's all right if it's us." So it was decided.

Inasmuch as we were all avowedly Against Everything, the question of presents was not even discussed. So when I got my next in-

---

AT WIT'S END:

Q: "WHY DON'T WE LIGHT THE
   HANUKKAH LIGHTS ALL AT ONCE
   ON THE FIRST DAY?"
A: "THE MIRACLE HAPPENED ONE
   DAY AT A TIME!"
— JERRY C., DECEMBER 2010

spiration I didn't even fight it. "I never said I wouldn't," I told myself, and plunged off into the depths of the Five-And-Ten, looking for jokes, odds, ends and trinkets that would fill two Christmas stockings. When I got it all home I had too much for the red mesh socks the Five-And-Ten doles out, but I remembered a pair of red tights someone had given me the year before (wrong size, unreturned) and I filled both legs, marked them "His" and "Hers" and put them under the tree, laughing immoderately. But on Christmas morning when I walked sleepily into the living room to start getting breakfast and saw the tree, the decorations and the "stockings," the whole effect brought me up short. Supposing they didn't laugh. Supposing Family Affair just got more depressed, supposing Nothing To Do got indignant. The doorbell rang. It was a little late to worry.

There they were: Family Affair, a little in the vanguard, a square package grasped firmly in both hands, obviously the spokeswoman. "I know how Against Everything we all are," she began, "but I happened to be in a hardware store and I know you need these and would never have the sense to go get them." She pressed the package on me. "It's not sentimental," she finished briskly, "it's coffee filters." Nothing To Do was more laconic. "Here," he said, handing me a small oil painting of bright spring flowers, executed and framed by himself. Since he is an artist by profession, this was quite a present. For one ghastly moment I felt my eyes filling with tears, but then, luckily, they both caught sight of my Christmas trappings in the living room. Following a stunned moment of disbelief, they burst out laughing. Breakfast was one of the highly successful social events of that season.

What came back to all three of us that year (the motor that started to hum again) was, of course, that much maligned X factor, the Christmas spirit. I didn't figure that out for myself. Another AA friend to whom I described our odd celebration, explained it for me. "It wasn't odd," she said, "it just worked because it was spontaneous. It was the spontaneity that made it. Nobody was obliged to do anything. There weren't any preconceived notions. Everybody just did what came naturally."

If joy eludes the noisemaker and cheerleader at your average party, real joy, alas, also gives a wide berth to the sulker, the foot dragger, the complainer and the worrier. There seems to me now no more point to being joyless on December 25th than to wake up and deliberately encourage a bad humor on any other day of the year. Christmas holds the same promise as a faultless spring day. And the same goes for New Year's Eve, Labor Day, the Fourth of July, your anniversary, my birthday. You never know until you go out to meet it what any given day is going to be, but the way you go to meet it surely makes a difference. As we all remember from experience, a change in attitude can have effects more radical than a change in external circumstances.

And so, dear Recently Divorced and dear Recently Sober, though I know how Against Everything we all are—the very best of us, at moments (and yes, these are "tricky times" for us)—still, we are also for the joy of living or we wouldn't be here, wouldn't have picked up this magazine to read, wouldn't know it existed. The Christmas spirit is just another evidence of that joy. So why fight it? Let go and let Santa Claus.

To the rest of the membership who are galloping full tilt toward the holidays, arms outstretched to embrace it all, I say, "Wait for me this year—I'm coming too!"

E. M. V.
Quogue, New York

COLD TURKEY
November 2009

I had received an appointment to teach at a very prestigious boarding school in the Midwest. I was assigned to teach literature, oral and written critique, competitive public speaking and competitive debate. My wife and infant daughter accompanied me, and we were ready to take on the world! I fantasized about being appointed headmaster of the school, and there appeared to be no obstacle big enough or complex enough to stop me from pursuing that goal.

I put in many long hours working with students after school, preparing for competitions. I encouraged the students to select one event and focus on that one event until the results of competitions (i.e., winning) indicated some mastery of the event. It seemed that we would be an unstoppable force if we continued to work hard and improve our competitive performance.

My teaching assignment blossomed with success. My home life, however, began to become interrupted a bit with my frequent headaches and hangovers from too much beer/vodka/scotch. It became harder and harder to get to school, cover up the odor of alcohol on my breath and clothes, and put enough eye-drops in my eyes to look like a "normal" person.

As fall turned into winter in my second year at this school, we approached Thanksgiving. I was drinking much more heavily, and it was harder and harder to function. On Tuesday of the week of Thanksgiving, my wife called me from work and reminded me that she needed some Thanksgiving dinner items—a turkey, some salad, olives, stuffing mix.

I went to the liquor store for a quart of vodka first and then spent the rest of our money buying dinner. Back home, I knew my wife wouldn't be home for another hour or so, so I opened the bottle of vodka, poured a healthy half-glassful, drank it and chased it with some pineapple juice. Just as I finished the pineapple juice, I heard the front door open. She was home early!

In my panic, I knew that I had to hide that bottle of vodka quickly, or we wouldn't have to worry about Thanksgiving. I quickly looked around the kitchen, couldn't immediately see any potential hiding place, and then spotted that turkey sitting in the sink. Holding the neck of the vodka bottle in my hand, I jammed it into the turkey carcass. I then opened the freezer and quickly settled the turkey into the back of the freezer as she walked into the kitchen.

"Yes, honey, I went to the store … No, I didn't buy any booze. I don't know why you always think I'm drinking."

She looked at me for about a full minute (try that sometime—a minute is a long time), turned around, and said she was going to take a little nap. I puttered around in the kitchen until she went to sleep.

Then, I crawled into bed and made sure that I was facing away from her. So far, so good.

When I had waited for about an hour in the dark, I was certain she was asleep. I quietly got up, went into the bathroom, washed my hands, brushed my teeth and turned the bathroom light off so that I could get readjusted to the dark. Certain that she was still asleep in the same position I had left her, I walked silently to the kitchen and, as quietly as I could, pulled the turkey out of the freezer.

I couldn't get the vodka out, though. It seems that the bird had frozen to the bottle, and it would be noisy to try to extricate it. So, being the clever fellow I thought I was, I just unscrewed the cap and took a straight swig from a frozen turkey's south end. Ahhhhh. That's what I like. One more swig, and I'd be able to sleep well. Here it goes, down the hatch! And at that moment, the kitchen light flipped on. My wife was standing in the doorway, looking wide-eyed at me "drinking" from our Thanksgiving turkey.

She divorced me in December. It took me five more years to accept what I secretly knew to be true: For me, drinking is not a matter of choice! I drink; that's who I am. When I found AA, I found the fundamental truth about myself—I am powerless over alcohol. I have no choice about drinking today or any other day. To stay sober, I would have to do something radically different. That radical difference occurred in 1981, when the police took me to a treatment center.

It has been 28 years since my last drink, and I can look back and laugh at the foolishness, cry over the losses and trust that my Higher Power will put in front of me exactly what I need to do today. I have friends, a wife, more children than I can keep track of and two kittens. We live with and work through real human relationships. We pray to a real entity that cares for me and mine in the same manner that I care for any of my 12 daughters and one son. And I've got a roomful of others just like me, who smile when I come in and who share with me their stories, strength and hope.

JIM L.
Newton, Kansas

HOLIDAYS, SHMOLIDAYS
November 2010

I've heard it said that among those who wanted to quit drinking, some found it especially difficult to do so around the holidays. I never understood that. What was so hard about quitting drinking on Groundhog Day, Flag Day or Boxing Day? With all seriousness though, these had about as much significance to me as any of the real holidays, like Thanksgiving, Christmas and Easter. They were just another day I felt compelled to consume alcohol in great quantity.

Having stepped into the realm of reality thanks to my re-discovered Higher Power—God—and the Fellowship of AA, I can now somehow envision the horror my wife and kids must have experienced the day of each new holiday. Here we go again, or, how drunk will daddy be today? they might have thought. And for good reason. I would often pre-drink, hiding it in the garage (the "war room" where I would strategize how to combat the world—my enemy) even though I would usually drive to the relatives' holiday party.

In retrospect, through the clear vision of today's sanity, my wife always drove home; not to do me any favors, but most likely to preserve her life and her children's. Imagine the nerve of her, assuming I couldn't drive just because I drank a 12-pack of beer and half a bottle of a strong liquor. After all, I had 30 years' experience of driving drunk with only one DUI, and that was not my fault; I was in the wrong place at the wrong time. Heck, I could drive drunk better than most people could sober. And besides, you'd drink and drive too if you had my relatives! This was the insane mindset of a man whose cognitive rationale was completely taken over by the disease of alcoholism.

Each and every time, this saint of a woman, whom I still admire for the courage to stand by this pathetic man whom she seriously didn't deserve, would pour me into the car after I miraculously staggered somewhere near it. Passed out most of the ride home, I would often wake up in the middle of the night still in the car. This was probably my wife's part, as I'm sure she was sick and tired of trying to wake me up to go into the house.

For most people, the holidays were a perfect time of reflection and thanks, punctuated with a celebration of a couple of drinks. This of course was the opposite with me. The holidays meant reflecting how the world had screwed me, and how you "normies" got all the breaks. So volatile were my thoughts of disdain and hatred that thankfulness was the last thing I possessed. I resented, with a passion, everything and everyone. I remember distinctly that every year when Thanksgiving rolled around I would get especially depressed, knowing that another year was going by and that I, still clueless about how to escape from my self-incarceration, was going to have to endure at least one more.

But for some reason, on Dec. 6, 2006, I relinquished the power of will (which I never had to begin with) to God and the Fellowship of AA. Almost immediately, I began using the tools (some of which I've always possessed) the program gave me, and discarded the one I was using my whole life: the shovel.

Today, when Thanksgiving comes around, I have a choice about how it will affect me emotionally. Today I choose to be thankful to have a mostly serene sobriety, with a new understanding for the holidays and what they really mean. Every day truly is a holiday, if you have the right spiritual awareness.

MATT S.
Buffalo Grove, Illinois

RULE 62 SAVES THE DAY
November 2001

On my first sober Thanksgiving, I'd been in AA only two months. It was a day my husband, two children, mother-in-law and I will never forget.

I began early in the morning to bake a turkey with the traditional trimmings and pumpkin pie for dessert. It felt strange to cook a big meal without the bottle of wine to accompany me and calm my nerves.

After the turkey had been in the oven for several hours, it became clear that something was wrong. There was heat from the upper coils, but the bottom of the oven was cold.

But we were resourceful. My husband took the turkey to his mother's apartment to finish baking while I continued with casseroles, bread rolls, and pie—all burned on the top and uncooked on the bottom.

When we finally sat down to eat late in the evening, we just skimmed our servings from the middle. Rule 62 saved the day. We were all laughing about the debacle, but everyone agreed it was our best Thanksgiving ever. Mom was sober.

ROSE K.
Monroe, Louisiana

BROKEN-DOWN CHORUS
December 2010

OK, guys, I've just got to share with you a wonderful thing that happened while my daddy was in the hospital.

Each year at my home group, we have a Christmas Eve dinner. I plan it, basically by default—I've just done it; someone has to. But this year has been very difficult because I've been in my daddy's hospital room in Birmingham, Ala., trying to plan this huge sit-down dinner for 35-40 people in Cullman, Ala. And, y'all, alcoholics, recovering with one day or 40 years, are a testy lot at best because they don't like rules, organization and being told what to do. Let's just put it this way: It's a delicate thing to make everyone think everything is their idea.

Anyway, there were wonderful people who helped decorate, lists were made, a turkey and a ham were cooked, people brought tons of food and God pulled this thing together. We had a ball.

Now, you're probably asking yourself, why is Gloria telling us this? It has to do with my daddy. Usually, Alcoholics Anonymous is anonymous, meaning that I usually don't disclose that I'm a recovering alcoholic. I'm not ashamed; I am grateful that I have found this way of living, but the problem is that if someone saw me drunk one day, I would want them to know that I failed, not AA.

Back to my story. The dinner was set for Christmas Eve. We do this because so many of the newcomers have burned so many bridges that an AA hall is the only place they have any Christmas at all. It's so important that they have someplace to go, to know there's hope, to receive love, to see people get better and to make amends to their families. Anyway, I, of course, was going to be with my daddy on Christmas Eve.

Daddy called me up and said, "Sugg, isn't that party supposed to be tonight?" I said, "Yes." Daddy said, "Gloria, I want you to go to that party and be there because AA saved your life and gave you back to me, and it's important to me that you be there for yourself and for the others." (Pretty long sentence for someone whom I didn't think really understood why I still go to four to five meetings a week after all this time.)

Y'all, I cried and I cried and I cried, and I went to the dinner. Now, everyone knew that my daddy was very sick and they wanted to know his progress and they told me that they'd pray for him. So nice. Anyway, I led the meeting and I told them what Daddy said. At the close, before we started the Lord's Prayer, I asked if I could call Daddy afterward so we could sing to him. They thought that was a great idea.

I called Daddy and said, "There's a whole lot of people up here who love you, want you well, and want to sing you a song." He started laughing as 25 broken-down drunks—who had found their way back into society and who could now hold their heads up thanks to the grace of such a merciful God—sang over my cell phone to Daddy, "We Wish You a Merry Christmas."

We sang and then clapped and then they all yelled that they loved him and wanted him to get better and come to the meeting in Cullman. As I hung up the phone, I could still hear him laughing.

I will remember this moment with my father until the day that I die. I just wanted you to know what God gave me for Christmas.

GLORIA G.
Cullman, Alabama

MY NAME IS SANTA C. AND...
(Excerpt)
December 1980

The wonderful thing I remember most about our Fourth Annual Holiday Alkathon in San Mateo County is that Santa showed up. He had his Christmas uniform on. He was smoking a cigar—which seemed out of character for Santa, but I'd seen many characters (from both Yale and jail) at AA meetings, so I didn't think too much of it. When the secretary asked if there were any new people who cared to introduce themselves, Santa said nothing. But when the secretary asked if there were any visitors from outside the area, Santa stood up and said, "My name is Santa C. and I'm from the North Pole."

The secretary then asked, "Are you an alcoholic?"

Santa replied, "You bet your bippy I am." We laughed and laughed. It made me feel so good to know that even Santa was one of us.

Our AA Fellowship has grown in leaps and bounds in San Mateo County, and the Alkathon has been a wonderful attraction during a holiday season that is difficult for a lot of lonely, still practicing alcoholics and for lonely sober ones, too.

L. I.
El Granada, California

CHAPTER EIGHT

"Are there any announcements?"

ONLY IN AA

AA characters, AA stories

Sobriety can be painful, it can be amazing, and it can be pretty darn amusing. Over the years, all of us in AA could write many volumes about the characters we've met (and become friends with), the adventures we've had, and the crazy stories we've heard. Much of it just has to do with accepting the things you cannot change, such as when a fellow member loudly breaks an AA's anonymity (with embarrassing detail) in front of a group of his coworkers in the story "Transfer, Please!" It's also about living life without going too crazy, as the woman who breaks her arm roller skating writes in "Whip it Good": "I wanted my partner to whip me around a corner. ... Like drinking, two turns were probably enough. ... The third turn ended in disaster." Here are just a few of the stories that you probably wouldn't experience anywhere but in AA.

A NIGHT TO REMEMBER
June 1998

I was a single man when I sobered up in 1953 and my sponsor was married with a family. Since he liked fishing, he thought it would be a good idea if I bought a boat. My sponsor was a very persuasive guy. The second year I had the boat, John, a tough old Nova Scotian I'd met in AA, wanted me to take him out for the annual big salmon derby. The first prize in this derby was ten thousand dollars, a small fortune in those days, especially for a couple of ex-drunks.

My friend John had been in the commandos during the war, and had later wound up in a Bordeaux jail on a murder charge. How he beat the charge I never did find out. I'd sailed with tough old characters like John during the war and done a lot of drinking with them in many parts of the world, so John and I got along just fine. I'm sure the people who are put into our lives in early sobriety do not show up by accident.

This little fishing trip turned out to be a barrel of laughs. The actual fishing time was to be on Saturday morning from six to noon, so John and I sailed out at five o'clock on Friday afternoon to a bay on the far side of a small island, just outside Vancouver. It was perfect weather, and as warm as a late August day can be in these parts. We arrived at the bay in about an hour and dropped the anchor. It was still light and we had the bay all to ourselves. We got the stove out and opened two cans of stew for dinner, with six slices of fresh bread and a large pot of coffee. We felt like millionaires. We sat back to watch the stars which were slowly becoming visible in the heavens. My boat was called "Serenity" and that night we were very glad to be sober and in our right minds. It was as if we'd never known any other life. The wild crazy life of drinking and bumming money to get more to drink was so far behind us that night, it was like it had happened in another lifetime.

While we were eating our dinner, we saw a large sailboat come into the bay and drop anchor on the far side, about a quarter of a mile away. The boat was over 75 feet long and had two masts and a jib, and it was a beauty. There were lights all over it and a party had already started. The revelers had a radio blaring away with dance music, and we could see about a dozen people on the deck. We looked over at the noisy bunch on board, and we knew they would be going at it for a few hours yet. We didn't care; nothing could have spoiled our tranquility that night.

We could hear almost every word that was said on the sailboat since the voices carried across the water. Then the fun began. A small dinghy took off from the shore and slowly made its way out to the bigger boat. When it got there, we could hear people say, "Hey, here's good old Bill. Come on board, Bill. Someone get Bill a drink. Yippee, glad you could make it, Bill!" Another voice bellowed out, "Come on, Bill, down the hatch, you've got to catch up to the rest of us." Then the music started up again, and everyone seemed to be singing as loudly as they could while a few were dancing some kind of jig.

An hour later we heard the music suddenly stop. A guy with a loud voice said, "Bill, you rotten son of a so-and-so, get your paws off my wife's leg or I'll throw you overboard." Someone else yelled, "The stinker was trying the same thing a minute ago with Joe's wife, while he was below. I think we ought to string the rotter up." Another voice said, "We ought to string him up to the yardarm. Let's teach him a lesson he won't forget." There was suddenly a lot of commotion on the deck of the sailboat. It looked like they were chasing somebody around, and it was most likely Bill.

Good old Bill grabbed a lantern and threw it at his pursuers. The oil lantern crashed down on the deck and started a small fire, and that took their minds off Bill for a minute. He made a dash for the rope ladder, which was still hanging over the side and he got nearly down to the dinghy before the others spotted him.

The people on deck started to throw beer bottles at Bill. He was trying to untie the rope that held the dinghy to the ladder and dodging beer bottles at the same time. He finally pushed the dinghy away from the ladder and started the motor. The ones on deck were screaming obscenities at him, and he was screaming right back at them. What a bloody fiasco! The dinghy gradually disappeared into the darkness. John and I were laughing our heads off. This was a better comedy than either one of us had ever seen in the movies, and this was real. All the excitement over Bill's arrival and sudden departure deadened what had been a lively party. The people on the sailboat eventually went below and quiet settled over the bay.

At five the next morning, John and I got up and made a big feed of bacon and eggs with toast, then we drank down a whole pot of coffee. We started to fish at six and kept trolling in the area till noon. We went past the sailboat about three times, but no one was stirring aboard. At noon the derby was over and still no one was moving on the sailboat. Both John and I knew exactly how they felt. We hadn't caught one fish but we still felt a million times better than they did.

John got married a year later and for two more years he was sober, then something happened and he got drunk. A month later, he was found dead in some downtown flophouse. I still think of my old friend once in a while, and my mind always goes back to that night they were going to string up good old Bill from the yardarm. He and I told the story many times and had a lot of laughs over the antics that had gone on that night. It's been over forty years and I still think of the sobriety John and I shared that starry night.

NEWTON B.
White Rock, British Columbia

WHIP IT GOOD *(from Dear Grapevine)*
November 2007

I have done some crazy, exciting things in sobriety—all new behaviors, for me. Before I found AA, I was never any fun. So, roller skating was a new fun thing to do. "It's like riding a bike," someone said to me as I wobbled onto the rink. I thought, I can ride a bike.

I'm not the type to give up just because I am not good at something. So I kept going around the rink, and each time I improved. It was fun. The last time around, I got carried away. Skating was okay, but I wanted my partner to whip me around a corner. I couldn't help it—I loved it. I laughed so hard that it took the rest of the lap to catch my breath. I was having a lot of fun, but like drinking, two turns were probably enough. I got a feeling that three would be too many, but this did not stop me. The third turn ended in disaster. The whip was perfect, but I went down. I broke my wrist.

I have an enormous course load at school and several term papers due. I am now typing at one-fourth my typing speed. Could I have been happy just skating like other people, or did I really have to have the "whip"? Even when I realize that there may be severe consequences in response to a reckless activity, it doesn't seem to enter my mind when I am in the moment. But I will not forget this anytime soon.

MICHELLE C.
Sonora, California

HI, WADE)!
October 2010

This story is rather humorous and shows how things can happen with regard to our anonymity. I recently had a get-together, or party, if you will, and I invited a number of friends. These friends brought some of their friends and the theme was a potluck and an evening where some of my fellow AA members played music.

The crowd was a mix of Alcoholics Anonymous members and "regular" folk who did not necessarily know one another. Some of the people who knew me knew I was in AA. Many did not, though, and I was speaking with a coworker who said he noticed that the punch was nonalcoholic, and that many of the people present that evening were not drinking alcohol. He also observed that those people seemed very happy and friendly. It seemed like the perfect time to tell him I was a member of Alcoholics Anonymous and that many of the people here that night were also members.

He proceeded to ask me which of the guests were also in the Fellowship. I explained that our Traditions did not allow me to point out another person's membership in AA, but that it was OK for me to tell him about myself. I told him that anonymity is the spiritual foundation of AA.

My friend seemed to understand. Soon after, one of the AA members proceeded to the stage to play a song. He made himself comfortable on the stool and began to tune his guitar. As he got ready to play he said to the crowd, "Hi, my name is Wade."

Half the people in the room turned to him in unison and said, "Hi, Wade."

My friend turned to me and said, "I guess I know now!" We had a good chuckle and the night went on to be one of the best many of us have had in sobriety.

JOE H.
Vancouver, British Columbia

STORY TELLERS ANONYMOUS
April 1973

For a long time, when called on to speak in AA, I hesitated to repeat anecdotes or jokes I had heard others tell at meetings, looking upon them as the property of the original narrators. To spread someone else's material around before the owners had a chance to do so themselves seemed like stealing.

But with time I have realized that the only plagiarism in AA would be to appropriate another person's drunkalog by relating it as if it had happened to me. Once someone has delivered a quotable aphorism or offered a meaningful parable at a meeting, it belongs to all of us; nobody has a copyright on it. Whatever will lift another member's spirits, clarify his thinking, or give him comfort becomes a communal possession. Hard as this may be on individual pride of authorship, it's all part of the slogan "You can't keep it unless you give it away."

One of the funniest accounts of "what we used to be like" is a story I heard at an Al-Anon meeting. Often, in describing our own past behavior, we alcoholics cannot do it justice, because we weren't really there; but a clearheaded, sharp-eyed spouse often was all too painfully aware of the whole scene.

In the interest of anonymity, I shall call this wife "Jane" and her Drinking Problem husband "D. P.," and designate the other two characters involved "Mr. and Mrs. Friend." The setting is California.

One Saturday morning, D. P. made a call on the Friends, during which he and Mr. Friend partook of the famous "couple of beers." When D. P. came home, he announced that the two couples were going to drive to Clear Lake that afternoon, and that Jane, since she had become so unreasonably fussy about riding in cars driven by people who had had "a couple of beers," could do the driving.

"Why Clear Lake?"

"The Friends have bought some property there and want us to see it."

"I'll think about it," Jane said.

In a few minutes, Mrs. Friend telephoned cheerily. "D. P. said you'd drive."

"Oh, did he?" So far, Jane had not made up her mind; but at that point, she did. "All right, I'll go, and we'll take my car. But on one condition—that there will be no backseat driving. Whatever I do, I don't want you or anybody else to say one word."

Somewhat taken aback, Mrs. Friend agreed. "Why, of course, dear."

So the two couples got into the car, the men in the back seat with a bottle to see them through the rigors of the journey, the two women in front. When they pulled onto the street, instead of turning right, in the direction of the freeways which would take them to Clear Lake, two hundred and fifty miles to the north. Jane turned left, toward the highway which went over the mountains to Santa Cruz, twenty-five miles to the south.

The men, laughing and talking in the back seat, paid no attention;

and Mrs. Friend, cowed by the condition she had accepted, made no comment.

When they reached the seaside city of Santa Cruz, Jane pulled up at a motel on the beach, went in, and registered, and the couples retired to their rooms.

D. P. walked out on the balcony, gazed across the vast expanse of the Pacific Ocean, said "Damn, that's a big lake!," turned around, came in, and lay down on the bed and slept the rest of the afternoon.

As Jane remarked at the Al-Anon meeting, "Why should I drive two hundred and fifty miles? He never did know we didn't go to Clear Lake."

The following story was told by the schoolteacher who figures in it. A little boy named Joey, who was about ten and inclined to be overweight, was habitually late for school. The teacher had chided him about it; notes had been written to Mamma and Papa, who had thereupon discussed the problem with their son; the principal had had heart-to-heart talks with Joey; yet one day the teacher glanced out of the window after classes had begun and saw Joey stumbling across the fields, one shoelace untied, sweater sleeve dragging, books being dropped, shirttail flapping. When, flushed and sweating, Joey entered the room, the teacher remarked, "I see you're late again."

"I know, Mr. S——," Joey replied seriously. "I thought about it this morning. You may not like it, and my mother and father may not like it, and the principal may not like it; but I've decided I'm going to get here when I can."

More than once, when the routine of my life has erupted into so many demands, tasks, and obligations piling up to a deadline that I feel as if I'll never make it, I have thought of Joey's "I'm going to get here when I can." And the smile it brings to my lips takes the heat off sufficiently to allow me to plod along in a more relaxed manner until, sure enough, I get there eventually.

The third anecdote I want to give away is one I dutifully kept to myself for over a year, because it was so good that I didn't want to steal the original teller's thunder. But apparently no one else thought the tale was worth stealing, for I've never heard it repeated.

This one happened on a South Pacific island during World War II. The American military outfit stationed there planted extensive vegetable gardens to supplement their diet. Everything did well, except cucumbers. The plants flourished and blossomed, but never bore cucumbers. Finally, the commanding officer wrote the Department of Agriculture in Washington to ask why the plants were acting like this. A botanist wrote back that only one species of insect carried the pollen to fertilize the blossoms, and that in the particular island our friends were occupying, there were none of those insects. Hence—no cucumbers.

So the CO called in a young private, equipped him with some cotton swabs, and sent him forth to do the insects' job. As the soldier painstakingly transferred pollen from one flower to another, a VIP who had flown in to inspect the post passed on his rounds with a retinue of officers and paused wonderingly to watch the private, who—with some embarrassment—continued his assignment.

Finally, the Big Brass demanded, "What on earth are you doing?" The soldier patiently explained the case of the unfertilized blossoms. "That's very interesting." After a thoughtful moment, the VIP inquired seriously, "And after you've done that, then what happens?"

"I don't know, sir," the soldier said. "From there on, you'll have to ask God."

I am sure a botanist could have given an answer to the VIP, and a biochemist could have added further information, and a physicist, even more. But I am equally sure that eventually human knowledge of what was going on in the cucumbers would have run out, leaving more questions unanswered. To me, everything that man hasn't found out yet and may never find out, because of his own limitations as one of nature's products, is what people call God. For me, this young soldier put it very neatly.

B. M.
Saratoga, California

NINETY-NINE YEARS
OF SOBRIETY *(from Dear Grapevine)*
August 1998

M any years ago, on the occasion of my fourth AA birthday celebration, a friend who shares the same sobriety date as mine dropped by our house and gave me a box of chocolate candy. My mother, who was eighty-five at the time, found the candy the next day and ate over half of the box. When I got home from work and discovered that seven of the twelve pieces were gone, my mother spoke up and said, "I ate it." I said, "Mother, don't you know that I received that as a gift for my anniversary of staying sober for four years?"

She replied, "Well, I've been sober for eighty-five years and no one has ever bought me a box of candy." Mother always had a sweet tooth.

This event took place back in 1979. I now have eighteen years of continuous sobriety. My mother lived until she was ninety-eight years, eight months, and eleven days old—I guess she had almost ninety-nine years of sobriety.

KEN J.
DeKalb, Illinois

HEARD AT MEETINGS
March 2007

A t an AA meeting, we took turns reading out of the Big Book. One member's turn came, and she read: "And now about sex. Many of us needed an overwhelming there." The woman (and her husband) got very red in the face. The room erupted in laughter.

JEFF H.
Pauls Valley, Oklahoma

GOING COLD TURKEY?
(*from Dear Grapevine*)
December 1983

A hunter had been after wild turkey for years with no success. One day, though, a turkey walked blindly up to him, and he promptly shot it.

The wild turkey is elusive game, with uncanny sight and hearing, and the man suspected the bird was injured or diseased. Close examination proved neither was true, but on dressing the bird, the hunter found it full of fermented grapes. The turkey was drunk!

D. R.
Corning, New York

TRANSFER, PLEASE!

July 1953

It had been a really serene morning and lunch with Les, our secretary, had given me a feeling of contented smugness. In the bus I settled down to return to the office, when I recognized a series of familiar greetings from the firm's secretary, sales manager, accountant and production chief, who occupied seats in the front and rear of me. I acknowledged their greetings, lit a smoke and waited for the bus to move off.

"So!—smoke with the flies, Pat?"

A voice and perfume thudded next to me. It was Anne and there was no mistaking that brandy-burr that sobriety had never eradicated in her penetrating tone. Uncomfortably I pacified her with a cigarette.

(Anne was dry. True, when the novelty had worn off she did give it a bang spasmodically for a week or more. Fast and furious was that binge and it shook many AAs. The funny part of it was that it didn't shake Anne. To her it was a demonstration, especially for others, of what she could be like when tanked up and also it silenced the critics who'd said that she used other stories dressed up differently to impress her audience.)

She skirmished around the weather, expressed indignation about the speaker at a meeting she attended, and as the bus moved, the pace and pitch of her voice increased.

"Was talking to a quack last night—about you!"

"Really?" I parried nervously in a hushed voice, praying that Anne would imitate. Not a chance—she increased her volume.

"Oh, yeah, this quack said, 'What! That soak sober! No, I simply cannot believe that he's sober!'"

The conductor was alongside for fares. I mumbled the amount in anguish, while she carried on relentlessly.

"Yep, I told the doc you'd not had a snort for five years and he said that was a miracle as you were the biggest drunk that was in Cape Town—and no human could cure you of your terrible thirst!"

I was becoming desperate as the tirade continued. This seemed to be a vault with Anne's voice reverberating around the tomb's silence. In my rapid glance toward the conductor for my change, I saw he was grinning. My imagination supplied the facial expression that must have been on my chiefs' faces. I dared not look in front or around. Desperate, I whispered softly:

"I don't recall the doctor you're speaking about."

"That's to be expected," she yelled, "You were always paralytic drunk when you saw him!"

Mercifully my bus-stop arrived. Crimson, I slunk up and croaked my farewell as I commenced to crawl down the corridor, my chiefs ahead of me.

"Oh! I haven't finished yet." Anne glanced around disappointed, but not to be outdone, she shouted after me:

"I told the quack that you, like me, had joined Alcoholics Anonymous!"

That is why I have lunch in the office these days and read the Serenity Prayer over and over. I also use the back entrance of the firm and will do so until my wound has healed.

P. J. O'F.
Cape Town, South Africa

UP IN SMOKE
June 2006

At 22 months sober, I'm still a baby to the AA way of life. One concept I can fully comprehend, however, is our purpose as a group. We help one another recover from our alcoholic insanity and grow emotionally, spiritually, and physically, by using the tools from the program. I experienced one neat tool recently:

After a recent Sunday morning meeting, I went home for my usual fix of pro football. I got a phone call inviting me to a character defect burning. I copied down the directions—even though I intended to stay home and watch three football games (one is never enough).

Halfway through the second game, I started thinking about my sponsor's comments on defects of character. After 31 years of sobriety, he says that he still has all of his. He laughs when he hears people say they're working on their character defects, because the idea is to not let them work on you.

Hey! Just like that, I was out the door, into the truck, and headed for what I figured, at the least, would be a campfire and some fellowship.

I followed the directions to a dirt road, went through a stretch of pine trees, and came to a lake with a sand beach surrounded by woods. It was about an hour before dusk. A small fire was already started.

Off to the left, not very far, was a tree much larger than the other trees. Someone tacked a sign on it. It read: TREE OF WILLINGNESS. Under the tree, there were logs and pieces of lumber of all sizes. All had blank sheets of paper stapled to them.

There was an instruction sheet on a nearby table. It said to pick out a piece of wood according to the size of the defect you wanted to get rid of, or the resentment you were trying to let go of, and write the defect's name on the paper. Offer a prayer to your Higher Power, throw the log on the fire, and turn your defect or resentment over to God. The instructions also carried this warning: "Be careful with your resentments, they may cause sparks."

When the sun set behind the trees in the west, a full moon rose above the opposite side of the woods, lighting up the lake as our bonfire grew.

Someone brought marshmallows. There were also conga drums, bongos, tambourines, a flute, and a guitar. We played, sang, and danced most of the night, and even cracked a few jokes about the concepts of AA as a cult. It was a great time. It was a sober time with family.

But, for me, the greatest feeling at the event was watching my particular character defect burn and turn into ash. It hasn't bothered me

for over a week now. Do I think it's gone forever? Probably not. But if—
or when—it rears its ugly head again, I'll know, deep down, it's spent
and can't burn me.

JASON B.
Del Haven, New Jersey

THE TWELVE STEPS

1. We admitted we were powerless over alcohol—that our lives had become unmanageable.
2. Came to believe that a Power greater than ourselves could restore us to sanity.
3. Made a decision to turn our will and our lives over to the care of God *as we understood Him*.
4. Made a searching and fearless moral inventory of ourselves.
5. Admitted to God, to ourselves, and to another human being the exact nature of our wrongs.
6. Were entirely ready to have God remove all these defects of character.
7. Humbly asked Him to remove our shortcomings.
8. Made a list of all persons we had harmed, and became willing to make amends to them all.
9. Made direct amends to such people wherever possible, except when to do so would injure them or others.
10. Continued to take personal inventory and when we were wrong promptly admitted it.
11. Sought through prayer and meditation to improve our conscious contact with God *as we understood Him*, praying only for knowledge of His will for us and the power to carry that out.
12. Having had a spiritual awakening as the result of these steps, we tried to carry this message to alcoholics, and to practice these principles in all our affairs.

THE TWELVE TRADITIONS

1. Our common welfare should come first; personal recovery depends upon A.A. unity.
2. For our group purpose there is but one ultimate authority—a loving God as He may express Himself in our group conscience. Our leaders are but trusted servants; they do not govern.
3. The only requirement for A.A. membership is a desire to stop drinking.
4. Each group should be autonomous except in matters affecting other groups or A.A. as a whole.
5. Each group has but one primary purpose—to carry its message to the alcoholic who still suffers.
6. An A.A. group ought never endorse, finance or lend the A.A. name to any related facility or outside enterprise, lest problems of money, property and prestige divert us from our primary purpose.
7. Every A.A. group ought to be fully self-supporting, declining outside contributions.
8. Alcoholics Anonymous should remain forever nonprofessional, but our service centers may employ special workers.
9. A.A., as such, ought never be organized; but we may create service boards or committees directly responsible to those they serve.
10. Alcoholics Anonymous has no opinion on outside issues; hence the A.A. name ought never be drawn into public controversy.
11. Our public relations policy is based on attraction rather than promotion; we need always maintain personal anonymity at the level of press, radio and films.
12. Anonymity is the spiritual foundation of all our traditions, ever reminding us to place principles before personalities.

AA Grapevine

AA Grapevine is AA's international monthly journal, published continuously since its first issue in June 1944. The AA pamphlet on AA Grapevine describes its scope and purpose this way: "As an integral part of Alcoholics Anonymous since 1944, the Grapevine publishes articles that reflect the full diversity of experience and thought found within the A.A. Fellowship, as does La Viña, the bimonthly Spanish-language magazine, first published in 1996. No one viewpoint or philosophy dominates their pages, and in determining content, the editorial staff relies on the principles of the Twelve Traditions."

In addition to magazines, AA Grapevine, Inc. also produces an app, books, eBooks, audiobooks and other items. It also offers a Grapevine Online subscription, which includes: new stories weekly, AudioGrapevine (the audio version of the magazine), the Grapevine Story Archive and the current issue of Grapevine and La Viña in HTML format. For more information on AA Grapevine, or to subscribe to any of these, please visit the magazine's website at www.aagrapevine.org or write to:

AA Grapevine, Inc.
475 Riverside Drive
New York, NY 10115

Alcoholics Anonymous

AA's program of recovery is fully set forth in its basic text, *Alcoholics Anonymous* (commonly known as the Big Book), now in its Fourth Edition, as well as in *Twelve Steps and Twelve Traditions, Living Sober,* and other books. Information on AA can also be found on AA's website at www.aa.org, or by writing to:

Alcoholics Anonymous
Box 459
Grand Central Station
New York, NY 10163

For local resources, check your local telephone directory under "Alcoholics Anonymous." Four pamphlets, "This is A.A.," "Is A.A. For You?," "44 Questions," and "A Newcomer Asks" are also available from AA.